30 Insights for New Teachers to Thrive

30 Insights for New Teachers to Thrive

Curt Richards

ROWMAN & LITTLEFIELD
Lanham • Boulder • New York • London

Published by Rowman & Littlefield
An imprint of The Rowman & Littlefield Publishing Group, Inc.
4501 Forbes Boulevard, Suite 200, Lanham, Maryland 20706
www.rowman.com

86-90 Paul Street, London EC2A 4NE

Copyright © 2023 by Curt Richards

All rights reserved. No part of this book may be reproduced in any form or by any electronic or mechanical means, including information storage and retrieval systems, without written permission from the publisher, except by a reviewer who may quote passages in a review.

British Library Cataloguing in Publication Information Available

Library of Congress Cataloging-in-Publication Data
Names: Richards, Curt, author.
 Title: 30 insights for new teachers to thrive / Curt Richards.
 Other titles: Thirty insights for new teachers to thrive
 Description: Lanham, MD : Rowman & Littlefield, [2023] | Summary: "This book provides a mixture of practical situations that every teacher, new or veteran, will face"-- Provided by publisher.
 Identifiers: LCCN 2022053090 (print) | LCCN 2022053091 (ebook) | ISBN 9781475871227 (cloth) | ISBN 9781475871234 (paperback) | ISBN 9781475871241 (ebook)
 Subjects: LCSH: First year teachers. | Teacher effectiveness. | Mentoring in education.
 Classification: LCC LB2844.1.N4 R54 2023 (print) | LCC LB2844.1.N4 (ebook) | DDC 371.14/4--dc23/eng/20221114
 LC record available at https://lccn.loc.gov/2022053090
 LC ebook record available at https://lccn.loc.gov/2022053091

This book is dedicated to my wife, India, and my daughters, Aaron and Whitney. Thank you for putting up with my many years of lesson plans, grading papers, and discussing gross topics at the dinner table. I love you all.

Contents

Acknowledgments ix
Introduction: The Heart of a Teacher xi

Insight 1: Monitor and Adjust. 1
Insight 2: Classroom Management: Rules and Corrections 5
Insight 3: Teaching to Various Learning Styles 11
Insight 4: Everyone Learns at a Different Rate 15
Insight 5: Make the Material Relevant 19
Insight 6: Consider the Needs of the Student. 23
Insight 7: The Teachable Moment: Time to Be Flexible. 27
Insight 8: Be a Servant Leader. 31
Insight 9: There Is Something Very Important about a Name. 35
Insight 10: Timing Is Important. 39
Insight 11: Help Build a Better Brain through Repetition and
Spacing. 43
Insight 12: Forgetting Has Its Place in Learning 47
Insight 13: Curiosity and Gap Instruction. 51
Insight 14: Teaching Machines versus Humans 55
Insight 15: Journaling Has Its Place in Any Subject. 59
Insight 16: Front Door–Back Door 63
Insight 17: Peer Learning: Each One, Teach One. 65

Insight 18: Teacher-Centered versus Student-Centered. 69
Insight 19: Use Your Teaching Energy Wisely and Stay Healthy. . . .73
Insight 20: Redirection versus Rejection. 79
Insight 21: Develop More Than One Passion 83
Insight 22: Stay Current 87
Insight 23: Classroom Organization and Displays. 91
Insight 24: Professionalism. 95
Insight 25: Nonverbal Cues 99
Insight 26: Documentation 103
Insight 27: Parent Conferences 107
Insight 28: Teacher Burnout and Rewiring Your Brain 111
Insight 29: Morning Person 115
Insight 30: Relationships with Fellow Teachers 119

Appendix A: Insightful Teacher Experiences 123
Appendix B: Always Remember. 139
About the Author 149

Acknowledgments

Thank you to my friend, fellow educator, and editor, Lorraine Angel. This project would never have happened without your insights!

Introduction

The Heart of a Teacher

WHY ARE YOU A TEACHER? THIS IS THE MOST IMPORTANT QUESTION that you must answer. In order to discover the answer, it is imperative that you realize the source of your passion. Do you love the subject or grade level you will be teaching? Do you have a passion for working with young people?

To love your students and love your craft is the fundamental philosophy of teaching, which comes directly from the heart of the teacher. The art of teaching—yes, it is an art—requires a layering approach from the ground up. The foundation to build upon is to love your students and love what you do and what you teach.

You can study and apply all the brain science that research has to offer. You can sit in college classes and professional workshops and take volumes of notes about how to organize a classroom and how to present material. You can read a hundred "how-to" books on teaching and classroom management. You can scour the Internet and read all the teacher blogs available. You can even construct your lesson plans so that they correspond perfectly with state standards. But if you don't love what you do, love what you are teaching, and love who you're teaching, then you will never be a highly effective teacher, and the classroom is probably not the place you should be.

Can your craft and the love for your students be cultivated? The answer is a resounding YES! There is a direct connection between proper organization and delivery of material and a growing love for what you do and who you teach, basically a self-fulfilling prophecy. If you enter the teaching profession with an expectation to love your students and to love teaching, you'll respond with behaviors that support this philosophy. These behaviors will manifest in your lesson plans and classroom activities, as well as how you approach and respond to your students. Eventually, you'll recognize your immeasurable influence and your artful ability to help change lives in a positive way, cultivating a love for your craft and for your students.

The purpose of this book is to guide beginning teachers and to refresh veteran teachers on how to handle many of the situations that confront ALL teachers and to guide teachers toward a love for their craft and their students. If you have been in teaching and are not as enthusiastic or as effective as you need to be, this book will highlight the basics of the art of teaching, helping you to regain your footing. These insights for new teachers will help them navigate many of the predicaments that will arise during their years as educators. You won't find these insights peppered with fancy educational jargon. What you will find are realistic situations that all teachers encounter, and some food for thought about maneuvering through day-to-day classroom experiences.

Each Insight presented here includes important points to remember, and these statements are listed again at the end of the book for quick reference.

As of this writing, I have taught in several schools and at various levels for thirty-seven years. During this time, I have mentored many first-year teachers and over a dozen practice teachers. I tell you this simply to say that I have vast experience in the art of teaching, and I'm still learning and developing, both in my subject matter and in my skills as a teacher, which is exactly what an effective teacher does.

Remember: Teachers should always be lifelong learners.

After the insights presented in this book, there are several humorous accounts from my personal experiences, both as a student and as a classroom teacher. One thing that a new teacher must quickly develop is a sense of humor—not sarcasm, which has no place in the classroom because it is hurtful. I kept a notebook in my desk and jotted down many of the funny experiences as well as poignant moments throughout my career.

Each year that I teach brings a deeper love for my students and my craft. You have chosen a noble profession. The effects of your influence will be far greater than you will ever know.

Every student has a story to tell. Every student has a life outside the classroom. Some of their lives are very different from yours. For this reason, you need to get to know your students and learn from them. Learn to love the diversity that they bring to your class. Your students will make you think differently about life and how people live because their world may be quite different from your world and how you were raised. That's okay. Their world is not your world. Learn to listen to them and you can truly make a difference in their lives.

Honor and love what you do and those you teach. Trust that you have made an impact on your students' futures.

Remember: No seed ever sees the flower.

In a completely rational society, the best of us would be teachers and the rest of us would have to settle for something less, because passing civilization along from one generation to the next ought to be the highest honor and the highest responsibility anyone could have.
—Lee Iacocca

Insight 1

Monitor and Adjust

EFFECTIVE TEACHERS ARE PLANNERS AND ORGANIZERS BY NATURE. If anyone wants to find a gift for a teacher, they can't go wrong with an organizer booklet or calendar. Organized teachers separate their pencils from their pens and keep a rainbow assortment of colored markers. Feed that need for organization.

Because most teachers are natural organizers, any interference with the daily schedule is stressful and aggravating. But it's going to happen: There are going to be interruptions to your daily plans. You can count on it! The disturbances are not always from the students but from last-minute, unannounced school-wide activities. At this point you are expected to "monitor and adjust."

Because of their incredible ability to adapt, teachers will be around forever. According to Darwin's laws of natural selection, a species must be adaptable to the ever-changing environment or it will cease to exist. The classroom environment is one of these ever-changing entities. Truly, no two days are alike, and interruptions to your plans are the norm. As the educational leader, you will be forced to adapt in many ways. Here are just a few:

- Students' personal issues. As much as you need to feel in charge, often you have to adjust your plans around the baggage your students bring from home, lunchtime, or from their previous classes. You may have to stop and deal with an unruly student who had a bad experience at home or in his previous class. Sometimes it's the crying student whom you need to console. Maybe a sick student throws up in the doorway of your classroom. All of these situations demand your immediate attention and take away from your planned instructional time.

- Buses arriving late. You can't control this, and neither can the students. Adjust your plans as you wait for all students to arrive.
- Unplanned and unannounced school assembly programs *are* going to happen. These interruptions to your planned schedule will get on your very last nerve. Your creative skill kicks in and you quickly devise ways to handle the instructional time you have lost. There's no fighting it: You *will* be interrupted without warning. Learn to be flexible.

Another interruption to the smooth flow of instruction is the need to monitor and adjust your students' learning. As wonderful as your lesson plans may be, there are going to be times when the students are not grasping the concepts, no matter how well you have planned and delivered. This situation is one that demands your creativity: Three strategies to help students understand include having different students explain the concepts to the class, using analogies, or asking students to create a song that explains the concepts.

Remember: Always have a Plan B.

Your Plan B can consist of a variety of adjustments. It may be an abbreviated version of a longer, planned lesson. It could possibly be an impromptu review of a previous lesson or assignment that supports what you are now teaching. For some grade levels, it could involve reading a favorite story to the class. The point is that when planning a day or even a week's lessons, take some time to create some alternate assignments and keep them in the pocket of your organizer.

The best Plan B strategy is something that can be plugged into a shortened class, no matter the topic you have planned for that day. It is obviously best if your alternate plan is related to the day's topic, but in the case of an extreme interruption of your class time, staying on topic is not always possible. You may need to postpone the concepts for the day and resort to your emergency plan to fill the time left after the interruption.

One advantage to having a "disaster plan" is that it can be retrieved and used at any time during the school year as well as in subsequent years. These activities are a teacher's gold.

Remember: There are going to be interruptions beyond your control, so close your eyes, take three deep breaths, and accept it. Then be prepared.

Insight 2

Classroom Management
Rules and Corrections

The kids who need the most love will ask for it in the most unloving way.

—Unknown

Every effective teacher knows that a well-planned and well-managed classroom decreases the probability of behavioral problems. If you keep the students on task with meaningful activities, most behavior problems will be kept to a minimum.

Busy work just for the sake of keeping students occupied can create problems in itself since they know when your sole purpose for an assignment is simply to keep them busy. You create behavioral problems by giving the students non-guided activities only so that you can sit and grade papers.

Remember: Teachers cause most behavior problems.

You need to be engaged with your students, not only to enhance learning but also to decrease the chances of behavior problems. Behavior of any kind is communication. A responsive, well-behaved student is our preference, but bad behavior occurs primarily when a student wants to get your attention or avoid doing something they don't want to do.

Remember: Negative attention is still attention, so beware of the amount of responses you give to students who aren't showing expected behavior. You never want to reinforce poor behavior.

Additionally, by trying to understand the source of the negative behavior, you may avoid reinforcing the behavior. There could possibly be underlying issues that manifest as behavior problems. Here are a few for consideration:

- Health concerns: Are there health concerns that need to be addressed? Is the student feeling bad or in pain? Does the student get proper sleep? Is he hungry or does he have low blood sugar? For post-puberty female students, are they having special issues that they find difficulty mentioning to a male teacher? To avoid the student feeling embarrassed, you can consult the school nurse or even a female teacher.
- Attention problems: Are learning challenges (such as ADHD or autism) present? The school counselor should have this information.
- Life situations: Has there been a change like sickness, divorce, abuse, or a death in the family in the student's home life recently?
- Academic misplacement: Especially in secondary school, students can be bored if they are not being challenged or they can be frustrated if they are in classes that are beyond their academic abilities.

All of these concerns must be considered when a student acts out or displays introverted behavior. None of these problems are a free ticket for students to behave however they wish, but if you suspect any of the items listed above, other professionals such as counselors, school nurses, or special education professionals should be consulted.

Remember: It takes a school village to educate a child.

When it comes to classroom rules, there are three basic categories of rules for students:

- School-wide rules: No classroom rule should usurp an established school rule.
- Safety rules: These may involve playground rules, laboratory safety rules, and other school safety rules such as those covered in fire drills, tornado drills, etc.
- Classroom conduct rules: These rules are your personal classroom rules. These are the type of rules addressed in this section.

Remember: Student behavior should never interfere with your teaching or a student's learning. Construct your classroom rules around this concept.

Don't inundate your students with tons of rules and consequences. You need only a small number of rules. If you build your classroom rules and expectations around the idea that students should never interfere with your teaching or someone else's learning, then your rules will be fair and easily understood. Your students need to understand the purpose of the rules, or many of them will see no point in obeying them.

Be sure to model the behavior you expect from your students. If you expect them to listen to you and to other students when they talk, then show that you listen to your students. If you expect your students to be on time to class, model punctuality yourself. Be organized if you expect organization.

Remember: Demonstrate positive behavior if you want your students to live up to your expectations.

Students will respond best when rules are written in the positive rather than the negative. You will get better results by telling students what behavior you expect rather than the behavior you don't expect. Also, be careful to make rules and consequences you can enforce.

Some basic classroom conduct rules might be as follows:

- Listen while the teacher or other students are talking.

- Be sure to bring all books and materials to class every day.
- Please keep your hands and feet to yourself.
- Stay on task.

Remember: The number one classroom rule should be "Please help me to teach and others to learn."

However, no matter how wonderfully you plan and how fair the rules are, there will be those few students who will push the limit. They're kids. That's their job. Allow them to question, but to question respectfully. The best way to get respect from your students is to give them respect.

Remember: Until you're a seasoned teacher, many of your students have had more years giving teachers hard times than you've had teaching.

Have *clear* and *fair* consequences that aren't aimed at punishment but correction when rules are broken. After all, it's not your duty to "get back at the rule breaker" but to correct, and hopefully change, the behavior by teaching the student why the behavior is not acceptable.

Be aware that some students will push you no matter how clear you have made your expectations. Once a consequence has been established, *don't back down*. Follow through with the correction.

Remember: You must be firm, yet flexible.

Never underestimate the power of parents in correcting more serious infractions and behaviors.

In your education classes and at administration-led teachers' meetings, the number one goal for classroom control is consistency, which sounds good on paper and in meetings, but it is not always possible to be totally consistent in every situation. Just as every student is not the same, every reason for breaking a rule is not the same.

There doesn't always have to be a one-size-fits-all correction. This doesn't mean that you shouldn't have clearly defined consequences for a rule infraction. Of course you should. Just keep an open mind to the individual circumstances.

Remember: To control, you don't have to be controlling.

For example, let's take a simple rule: *Please remove your hat when entering the classroom.* That's a very cut-and-dried rule. Either a hat is on the head or it's not. The standard consequence may be that the teacher takes the hat and the student picks it up at the end of the day. Sounds simple enough. But let's unpack this scenario. Maybe it's cold out and Johnny simply forgot his hat was on his head. You could discreetly point to your head and most likely he would remember his hat and remove it. Problem solved.

You don't have to place an emotional, embarrassing wedge between you and the student for the entire class period. Also, you don't have to expend the energy of waiting around for Johnny to show up at the end of the day to retrieve his hat.

However, if Johnny refuses to remove his hat or places it on his head immediately after taking it off, then you enter the new territory of correction. You get your best results by avoiding a confrontation in front of other students.

Never call out a student in front of the class; public humiliation is guaranteed to make a student hostile and resentful. Give the class a quick activity and ask Johnny to step outside the room or to the back of the room. The situation will usually be resolved if you are positive and explain your expectations. This approach sends a clear message that you care and that you want him to succeed.

It takes energy to make and enforce rules. If you're not careful, you'll spend an appreciable amount of time determining rules and the consequences of breaking those rules. This is precious time and energy that eats away at your educational creativity. That's not to say that you should create a "rule-free" classroom.

Make your rules education-centered and flexible. Obviously, some situations such as labs, PE classes, and school-mandated drills require specific safety rules. When the rule involves personal safety, there's not much wiggle room for error. At these times, you may need to be more assertive.

Remember: When rules are broken, it's not personal, so don't respond as if you've received a personal attack.

Insight 3
Teaching to Various Learning Styles

In their education classes in college, all teachers-to-be study the various learning styles. Some experts in this area have identified up to seven different learning styles, but generally, we consider only three main cognitive styles: auditory, visual, and kinesthetic. At the beginning of the term, some secondary school teachers conduct a Learning Styles Inventory for each student. These can be found online if you feel you need to go that way, but research doesn't necessarily support the accuracy of these tests.

Some educational researchers will tell you that teaching to the students' learning styles is outdated and inefficient. Attempting to discover a particular learning style for a student by administering a Learning Styles Inventory is not an effective use of your time and doesn't tell you much about a student's ability to learn. You can't concentrate on one style of instruction tailor-made to individual students; instead, the best results come from constructing your lessons to encompass *all* learning styles.

It's rare for a student to lean toward a single way of learning and processing information. It's true that some students will gravitate toward a particular instructional style; however, most learn from multiple instructional formats. The best practice is to conduct your lessons to incorporate many teaching techniques. If you design your teaching to cover all the styles listed above, an inventory is not necessary for the average class.

Insight 3

Remember: Understanding that most teachers tend to teach in the manner that they were taught, a teacher must be intentional about having auditory, visual, *and* kinesthetic learning styles.

Attempting to determine how your students learn is extremely important, but it is just as vital to analyze how you approach a subject. How do you tend to teach? We often tend to drift toward a comfortable style of instruction and, if we're not careful, we'll adopt a teaching preference based on our own personal learning style.

Think back over your own experiences in K–12 and college, and you'll realize that some, if not most, of your favorite teachers approached a lesson using a variety of techniques. Sadly, too often we remember the "bad teachers" who had only one style of instruction and showed little desire to vary their teaching approaches.

Remember: If a student is not learning from the way you teach, find out how they learn and change the way you teach. This might involve giving that student a Learning Styles Inventory.

When developing a lesson or course of study for your students, ask yourself one important question: *How much time is spent with me talking and the students listening?* Psychologists will tell you that most people's attention span for listening to someone talk is on average around fifteen minutes, if that much. Even this amount is not uninterrupted.

Researchers have found that continuous attention spans last about twenty seconds before the mind wanders. Of course, this time frame varies with the age of the student, interest in the subject, and the teacher's charisma or lack of appeal! Educators are finding that this continuous time frame is decreasing, because of information overload in our world.

Conduct a personal experiment. Watch a TV program with commercials. Try to count the seconds that a visual is on the screen before it switches to another frame. In most cases, it's barely two seconds. Our young people are being conditioned to receive information in increasingly smaller bites. So with this in mind, a teacher's lecture time and instructional time should be divided into shorter sections that involve a variety of learning styles.

Remember: Your delivery of information needs to be engaging, and perhaps entertaining, as well as brief.

This statement doesn't mean that you need to put on a "dog and pony show" every time you're instructing your students. To increase their attention span, you must make the material as relevant as possible. You may tell a few personal stories or invite them to offer their experiences related to the subject.

To elaborate, if a biology class is beginning a discussion about the skeletal system, the teacher could ask if anyone has ever broken a bone and have students identify which one. If you're presenting a lesson in geography or even history, you may tell a story about a trip you've taken to the area you're discussing. Of course, when students are invited to share their experiences, proper classroom management and your skill to keep on topic is vital so that the lesson doesn't spiral out of control and you're not "chasing rabbits."

The instructional portion of the lesson may be geared toward auditory learners, but you can tilt your lesson to the visual learners by the use of a computer presentation or some sort of model, demonstration, or display. The instruction should be interspersed with hands-on activities like drawing, model construction, and improvisational techniques, just to name three.

To integrate numerous learning styles, try to incorporate a multisensory approach that engages as many senses as possible. If you are teaching your students about various fruits, have them see, smell, and taste the fruits. Then have them write about what they have experienced and tell you about their experience. This activity allows the students' brains to use a variety of neural circuits such as tactile (touch), kinetic (movement),

Insight 3

olfactory and gustatory (smell and taste), as well as auditory and visual. This integration of the senses will allow the brain to enhance memory.

Remember: When designing a lesson, be sure to incorporate the major learning styles into your instructional plan.

INSIGHT 4

Everyone Learns at a Different Rate

As teachers, we would love it if our students hung onto every word we uttered and immediately understood every concept we teach; however, in the real classroom, you'll hear "I don't understand," quite often. This statement can be good to hear. First, you know the student is paying attention. Second, you know how you presented the material and that you need to adjust your explanation. How you handle your next statement might determine not only if the student understands the concepts you're teaching but also if they will ever learn anything else from you.

Remember: The only dumb questions are the ones that were never asked.

It goes without saying that you should never, ever belittle a student for asking a question, no matter how much you want to shake your head in disbelief. Your disrespect will not only lose that student for the rest of the course but probably most other students as well. Let the questioning student know that he has your full attention and that his question is of the utmost importance to you. It's at these moments when your true teaching ability can shine. These are the pure teachable moments, not just for the student, but for you as well—an exciting yet terrifying place to be. You are about to go off-book and improvise.

So where do you go from here? The first thing that you need to determine is why the student does not understand. Never discount the possibility that it is your fault. Did you speak too fast? Did you speak clearly? Teachers are public speakers. Practice enunciation and the proper speed of speech. Did you give too much information at one time? When you give instructions to your students, pause and check in with them to make sure they are with you. If a student does not understand the first instruction, then they will be lost in subsequent directions and concepts.

Remember: Always speak clearly and at the proper speed for students to understand.

Consider the rule of threes. Material usually stays with students best if they are given no more than three bits of information at a time. When you follow this rule, stop and check in with the class after three parts of instruction.

Simply repeating your previous explanation may not help. A computer tech working on a program that's not responding as desired will always return to the last working operation. Find out the last concept that the student understood and build from there.

In the brain, learning is boosted by detecting, connecting, and making patterns. We learn best when we link new knowledge to existing patterns in our brains. New learning must connect to what the learner already knows. As teachers, we help students to identify ways to fit new information into their existing knowledge patterns, which will aid their brains in developing more synaptic connections.

Remember: Always take a student from where they are to where you want them to be. Better yet, allow them to discover the path between old and new information.

When you have spoken on the phone, or even in person, to someone, have you ever misunderstood what they were saying? It's very irritating and quite senseless for that person to repeat the statement in the exact same words and tone. When a student doesn't understand a concept, it's your job to regroup and run at the problem from another angle. Don't repeat what they obviously didn't understand in the first place. Depending on the subject matter and age group, you may need to use simpler words, add an applicable drawing, or provide an analogy.

Remember: When students don't understand a concept, it might not be their fault.

You should not view learning as something difficult but as an adventure. As teachers, we're expected to lead students toward a mindset of growth. Students need to be reassured and shown that learning is attainable. One reason that some students have trouble following directions is because they have become accustomed to not understanding, or they simply decide beforehand that they will not understand. Attempt to build the students' confidence by assuring them that they will do well on this lesson.

The youngest students will realize that learning is not only possible, it's fun. Unfortunately, as middle school and high school approach, many students view learning as a challenging task, causing them to view themselves as limited in ability and intelligence. As a result, they will often adopt the philosophy that it's "cool not to care," since few want to be labeled as the "class nerd." This attitude is a defense mechanism that can be one of the most challenging mindsets for a teacher to overcome.

Your students need to experience a sense of accomplishment. In many situations, students are so used to failure that they come to expect it as normal. Therefore, it's very important for a student to taste success.

Remember: Teachers need to acknowledge their student's efforts, no matter how small.

Sadly, the school system often has reinforced this expectation of failure by requiring a barrage of standardized tests. We can't change the existence of state-mandated testing any more than we can rid a summer night of pesky mosquitoes, but we can structure our teaching as well as our evaluations so that success is attainable and learning is adventurous. We can help build natural interest and curiosity.

Remember: Human beings are built to learn.

Insight 5

Make the Material Relevant

A COLLEGE PROFESSOR ONCE SAID, "UNLESS YOU CAN TELL A STUDENT how the material you're teaching directly affects his life, you shouldn't be teaching that topic." This statement is a loaded sentence that needs some unpacking. First of all, you will most likely have state standards that will dictate most of your material, but there will be some "wiggle room" involved for you to insert topics that you feel are necessary.

The truth is that not every topic on your syllabus will directly influence the daily life of your students. They are expected to learn for the benefit of their futures and not only for their present lives. So which is it? Do we simply teach material that will have value for the students' immediate lives or do we lay the foundation for future courses?

Actually, it's both.

If you're teaching the Pythagorean theorem in math class, it's difficult to explain how this knowledge will change your students' weekend. But, teaching how to balance a checkbook or keep track of debit card purchases may impact their lives immediately, especially those of the older students.

A student once asked a teacher why he had to take algebra. He was going to be a professional football player and had no use for the subject. The teacher sidestepped the obvious fact that most high school football players never see the pros, since that fact wasn't the point. Too, the teacher didn't want to downplay the student's dreams, so she told him that he had made an excellent point. Then, appearing to change the subject, the teacher asked why lifting weights helped a quarterback throw a perfect spiral. The student's eyes widened, and he then began to expound on the importance of football fundamentals, which all begin with strength training. To that concept, the teacher slid in the idea that algebra could help improve reasoning ability that can be valuable in any area of life, even football. So even if the student didn't think he would use algebra in his career, by his studying it, he took his brain to the "brain gym" and improved his thinking skills. Who knows if the teacher convinced him, but the student did take algebra.

Many of the topics we teach have far-reaching effects by improving higher-order thinking skills. Reasoning ability is a tool that's useful in all areas of students' lives. So with that concept in mind, we can agree with the professor's comment; however, many of the topics we teach may appear to be stand-alone material that has no direct application to the students' lives at the moment. But the creative teacher can change that.

Teaching most subjects requires a layering process. The fundamentals must be mastered in order to move to the next level. We don't teach children the ABCs and never move on to word and sentence formation. We don't teach the periodic table without eventually discussing the bonding of elements to form molecules and compounds.

Remember: Learning is a building process.

An elementary math lesson on fractions is certainly applicable at home, where fractions are used every day in cutting a pizza or measuring portions in a recipe. A lesson in history doesn't have to remain in a particular century; often historical events set the scene for the present day. Students can apply a chemistry lesson in the garage, kitchen, or hair salon. The creative teacher can make real-world connections when presenting the subject matter, therefore making the lesson relatable. But don't be the only one thinking about how relatable a lesson is. Have the students explain some ways they could use the information in the lesson.

Remember: Students will respond best if they can relate to the material.

Make the Material Relevant

Students of any age love stories, especially personal stories from your own life experiences. Tell a humorous or possibly suspenseful tale that connects the topic of discussion to an event in your life. Students are curious about their teachers' lives. Since they often have a hard time imagining their teachers as real people with real lives, this might be all the motivation needed to sneak in a concept when you weave a tale about your own life. Your students will not only see the relevance of the lesson when you tell it from your personal point of view, but it can also give them a mental hook to aid in the retrieval of the concept at a later time.

You can satisfy the professor's philosophy by giving the student an idea of the relevance of the material, and if it can change their weekend, that's wonderful for both of you!

Insight 6

Consider the Needs of the Student

Most teachers who took educational psychology classes learned about Maslow's hierarchy of needs. These basic, social, and self needs are (from the lowest to highest levels) physiological (food and clothing), safety, love and belonging (friendship), self-esteem, and self-actualization. According to Maslow, people have a desire to be the best they can be, so the first needs in the hierarchy must be met before those needs higher on the list; in other words, physical needs must be satisfied before social needs, and social needs before those of self-fulfillment. You must consider these needs when you deal with students and as you design materials and activities for your classes.

Maslow's hierarchy sets the very base level needs as the physiological ones. A student's cognitive ability will not reach full potential until his basic physical needs are met. To help provide for the students' nutritional needs, the school system has programs in place such as lunch and possibly breakfast programs. These nutritional programs are not the teacher's responsibility, but there are classroom factors that are certainly in your control.

You can create a comfortable learning environment by being aware of several factors. The room temperature is one of these factors. Depending on your classroom situation, adjust the temperature the best you can. Providing a safe box fan for warm days or allowing the perpetually chilly student to keep a blanket or extra jacket in your room is feasible. You can increase the students' comfort by having a reasonable bathroom and water fountain policy. Many elementary schools allow for snack breaks during the day; having a class parent to help organize this process can be a wonderful addition to your program.

Secondary schools do not usually allow for snacks in the classroom, but it is important to know if any student is diabetic and needs to eat something during class. After you have verified the student's health status with a guidance counselor or parent, provide a private setting for the student to eat.

Remember: Students learn best when they are physically comfortable.

Safety is the next level of need. It goes without saying that students must feel physically safe in your classroom. School systems are constantly working to provide safe environments, such as by practicing various periodic drills. As a classroom teacher you must be mindful of any weak or broken chairs and tables and any equipment that is unsafe. In many districts the local fire marshal will have rules concerning extension cords and power strip placement, preventing electric shocks and anyone tripping over cords.

Special safety rules apply for science laboratories and gym classes. Enforce those rules with no exceptions. Too, schools that allow recess and playground time expect the teachers to be diligent in monitoring the students' activities while they are outside.

Remember: Teachers are expected to keep their students safe in the school building as well as on the playground and in common areas.

There is another essential aspect of safety that arises directly from your classroom management: emotional safety. Students must feel safe from embarrassment and ridicule from other students and from you. Students must feel that you are protective of their emotional state as well as their physical safety, and they should feel free to ask questions and be taken seriously. Too often teachers make comments to students that are hurtful, even if the comment was not intended to hurt or if it was thought to be a "joke." When a teacher makes a sarcastic remark, the student will retreat into himself and all learning shuts down. Be aware of your comments, body language, and your volume and tone of voice when you address your students. Also, make it crystal clear that you will not tolerate bullying and unkind comments from other students.

Remember: Students need to feel valued and respected in order to learn.

How you speak to your students will also reinforce the need for belonging. The best learning environment is one where the students enjoy being in your class and feel accepted, even if they don't feel like they are the best and brightest academically. If a particular student tends to be a loner with little or no interaction with other students, attempt to group him in activities with other students who seem to be inclusive by nature. You are not responsible for creating friendships between students, but you can observe your students' personalities and gently encourage less-involved students to become more active participants.

Remember: Create an environment of inclusion, not exclusion.

One of the best ways to help foster self-esteem is for your students to taste success. Always work to design activities and evaluations where everyone can have some degree of accomplishment.

Remember: Success builds self-esteem.

Having a student experience success may be as simple as asking free response questions of various difficulties and calling on certain students to answer the easy ones. Never think of a student's answer to a question as wrong but instead consider it incomplete. From that point you can guide him to the answer you were expecting.

If Johnny answers incorrectly, guide him further: "Ok, Johnny, good, I see where you're coming from. Now, what about . . . ?" Then lead him in the direction you intend for him to go. As stated earlier, always take a student from where they are to where you want them to be.

Self-actualization, as stated in Maslow's hierarchy, involves a person reaching his full potential. You can help with this process by recognizing individual talents that students possess and encouraging them to develop these abilities.

Self-actualization is not something that we can always measure or observe. But over the span of a school year, you can witness improvement in grades and attitude as well as apparent growth in self-esteem.

Remember: You can help a student's self-esteem, but it takes time. Be patient.

Understand that these hierarchies in education are not intended to be evaluated scientifically but to be used as a framework for student-teacher interactions as well as development of teaching strategies.

Insight 7

The Teachable Moment
Time to Be Flexible

The "teachable moment" is one concept that any college student in education courses hears many times. The phrase is tossed around in seminars and professional development courses, but as teachers we have a love-hate relationship with the idea. We have trained ourselves to be organized, efficient teaching machines. Any teacher worth her salt would never consider entering a classroom without lesson plans A and B tucked into her tote bag. The idea of moving away from the plans into the realm of "winging it" makes our palms sweaty. But this is where the "teachable moment" arrives.

Actually, it's preferable to refer to the phrase as the "learnable moment," since it's more student-centered than teacher-centered. It's that moment when you can almost see the light bulbs over the students' heads turn on and shine brightly. You finally witness the connections that the students are making. Pure learning has begun. Yet, making the observation is not the end product. Once you recognize the sprouting of the special moment, it's time to go off-book and nurture the growth. See the moment as an opportunity to make a difference.

The readiness of your students to absorb a particular concept is not entirely in your control. As teachers, though, we expect to be in control and may miss a wonderful opportunity if we're not willing to—at least momentarily—set our plans aside and engage our creativity in order to encourage the student.

Remember: The "learnable moment" may arise at any time. Allow yourself to be flexible.

Teachable moments are usually thought of as spontaneous flashes of insight from the student, but it doesn't always have to be this way. Often you can stimulate these special learning moments by offering a series of open-ended questions. By not giving the students too much information and by allowing them to discover where you are leading them, you have primed their brains for understanding.

During these moments of insight, the brain actually responds in a different fashion than during guided learning sessions. Clusters of neurons are enriched and the brain is flooded with dopamine, which gives a feel-good boost.

Interestingly enough, some areas of the brain that allow for distraction decrease their influences, allowing for full concentration. This may explain why we often close our eyes when we are trying to concentrate or remember some fact. Auditory stimulation, such as other students talking or even the teacher offering a lengthy explanation, can interfere with the brain's flashes of insight and attentiveness to a thought. If a student is obviously trying to arrive at an understanding, it is best to not inundate him with questions. Let him lead, since too much sensory information can distract him from making the connections his brain is attempting to create.

As a teacher, you're naturally observant, especially when it involves your students. After you respond to the "light bulb" moment from a student, it's time for you to have a "what, when, and how" moment of your own. When you have the chance to reevaluate your lesson and the way you handled the "Aha" moment, you make notes to yourself describing what you were doing when the breakthrough occurred and how you controlled it. Since lesson plans are ever-evolving, your notes may be valuable the next time the topic is discussed.

Sometimes these special moments are so unique that you may wish to share them with your colleagues who teach the same course or grade level. Your success can be a perfect topic for a departmental meeting or an online forum, opening a dialog where teachers explain the special impromptu events that have occurred in their respective classrooms.

Remember: Always record your successes for future use and share them with other teachers.

Insight 8

Be a Servant Leader

THE SERVANT LEADER IS A SIMPLE BUT PROFOUND CONCEPT THAT focuses on your attitude about your role as teacher. You are, of course, in charge of your classroom, but never think of yourself as being above the students. When dealing with students, one of the first things you need to do is take an inventory of your *own* personality, not an easy task. Any time we turn the mirror on ourselves, we stand the chance of discovering traits that we don't like.

Ask yourself some hard questions like the following ones:

- Do I have a controlling attitude?
- Have I ever been humiliated, and if so, what did it feel like?
- Do I tend to frighten students into submission?
- Do I overcompensate because of a lack of self-confidence?

After you have looked deeply into your own motives and found areas that need work, you are ready to respond honestly to your students.

Remember: At one time you were sitting where they are now, so think about how you are perceived by your students.

Your goal should be to serve your students as you lead them. In order to be a proper servant, you must be a proper leader, which involves a different attitude than many of the teaching models that you studied. To be a servant leader, you need to exhibit patience, compassion, empathy, and awareness. To achieve these traits as a teacher, you must first become a good listener and an astute observer of human nature.

Over half of the misunderstandings that occur in a classroom can be traced back to the poor listening skills of one of the parties involved. We automatically assume the student has an inadequate ability to listen, but very often it's the teacher who needs to improve her skills as a listener. Take time to hear what your students are saying with their words and their body language, which allows you the ability to develop the skills of hearing what they are *not* saying as well as what they *are* saying.

Remember: Be aware and listen to the nonverbal cues that students send you.

Becoming involved as a listener and an observer doesn't mean that you become your students' "friend" or "buddy." Honestly, they don't want you to be on their level. Students expect guidance and leadership from a respected person, but above all they want to be accepted and heard.

As teachers, we are talkers, and when we talk, we expect for someone else to listen. There is an old adage that says, "We were given one mouth and two ears, so listen twice as much as you talk," and it is a saying usually aimed toward students. But teachers need to heed it as well. When you show a genuine interest in your students' words and actions and thereby become aware of their needs and feelings, then you can begin to develop empathy and compassion for their personal lives. Your sincerity will encourage them to become open to what you are teaching.

Teachers become servant leaders when they notice the little things about their students. Is he feeling bad today? Is she upset about something? Hungry? Is he embarrassed about his clothes? There are no magic words or actions to deal with these issues. It's all on a case-by-case basis.

You are not going to fix all of your students' problems. As teachers, we have difficulty accepting that sometimes we are not able to find a solution to their problems. After all, we tend to be fixers by nature, but fixing problems is not your job. You simply need to develop trust. Many times, you'll be at a loss for words, and that's okay. Often, a student just wants you to listen and care.

Many problems will certainly be beyond your control and expertise, so consulting a school counselor on some of the more pressing situations is a wise decision. But the bigger point is that a servant leader is aware of their students' needs and cares enough to address their issues in the appropriate manner, even by simply listening.

Remember: When teachers listen to students' ideas, students can truly blossom.

Insight 9
There Is Something Very Important about a Name

A ninth-grade teacher was standing before her physical science class on the first day of school, calling the roll for the very first time, a nerve-racking experience for a new teacher. She made it through the list with only a few mispronunciations. Later that morning during her assigned lunch duty, a couple of students walked by, one of whom had been in the teacher's morning class. The young man looked at the teacher and spoke to her.

The teacher promptly responded with "Hey, Rodney!"

Rodney's eyes widened and a huge smile appeared on his face. As the students walked on, Rodney playfully punched his buddy on the arm and said, "She knows my name!"

It was at that moment this teacher realized just how important learning her students' names is to the teacher-student relationship.

Remember: Names may have some familial or historical significance. Take your students' names seriously.

To mispronounce a student's name or, even worse, to call a student by a name that they don't like to be called can drive a wedge between you and the student, a wedge that's difficult to remove. Depending on your school's location, non-Anglicized names are most often mispronounced. If you properly pronounce a name that traditionally gives teachers difficulty, you will immediately establish a bond between you and that student.

If you can get your roll ahead of time, it's always a good idea to practice proper pronunciation or consult with another teacher who may have taught some of your new students the previous year. If you consult another teacher, be careful, and do not allow that teacher to make negative comments about any student. Negativity will keep you from having an open mind concerning the student.

Let the students know that they're free to correct you respectfully or tell you a name they prefer to be called. A student feels important when you call them by their name because they realize that learning their name took effort and shows that you care.

From a biological perspective, the brain activates when someone calls our name out loud, releasing feel-good hormones such as dopamine and serotonin. The medial prefrontal cortex is responsible for many processes that are involved in self-identification and self-representation. This brain region tends to increase in activity when we hear our own name. Also, this is the same region involved in self-judgment. Hearing our names stimulates and primes our brains to learn.

It's a great idea to work in your students' names during your lecture or explanation time. Make it appear natural. The students don't need to feel singled out as if they were doing something wrong. Simply using their names as if you were conversing with them keeps them attentive and lets them know that you care enough to make sure they are listening and learning.

Remember: Using a student's name communicates respect.

One technique used by some master teachers is to have a cup of popsicle sticks with a student's name written on each stick. When you ask a question, ask the question first, wait ten seconds (important so that everyone has time to determine the answer), and then pull out a random stick and read the name drawn. If the student whose name is on the stick answers correctly, congratulate him and move on to the next question. If that student does not know the answer, tell him you will ask him again after you get him some help. Pull out another stick with a new name and ask that student the same question. If the second student answers correctly, return to the first student, call his name, and ask the same question.

This method keeps all students focused and responsible for knowing the material. It's important that you call every student by name every class period. This technique not only creates a sense of accountability for students but also enhances a level of comfort so that they feel at ease asking questions or requesting clarification of concepts.

Remember: Learn your students' names quickly, and use them often.

Insight 10

Timing Is Important

One question that practice teachers often ask is, "How do I know how much material to prepare for a class period?" Preparation and planning can certainly be a point of stress for any teacher, especially a new one. The longer you teach, timing a lesson is something you will perfect. It seems as if you either have too much material to cover in the time allotted or the material is going to run out with too much clock left in the class period. Planning with a time limit in mind is a balancing act that will be with you for your entire career, but it will get easier with experience.

Generally, it is best to prepare more material than you think you will need, but when you design your lesson compartmentalize the information: Using an oral or written list, declare a check time at which you stop and summarize or restate the covered material. Have your students silently or verbally check off if they understand the concepts. If you see that there's not enough time to complete a full lesson, you are not stopping midway through an idea. Now you have a starting point for the next class.

The goal, though, is to time your topics and stick to that timing so that you finish a lesson during that class period. If you explain clearly and concisely, your students probably won't be asking questions, which takes more time.

Remember: Never stop a lesson in the middle of a concept.

Throughout your career as a classroom teacher, have two open notebooks on your desk. One notebook contains your teaching notes and the other is your plan book with a bulleted list of material to cover during that class period. You can add to your planning list a few strategies for review and enrichment, just in case the stars align and everything goes smoothly with few interruptions and you finish the material early. (This happens, but don't get used to it!)

When the material seems to run out long before the clock, you can pull from your collection of personal stories related to the topic or ask the class about their experiences. Also, you can always spend the last few minutes on an impromptu review of what you have taught, using the popsicle jar mentioned in an earlier insight. Another way to review is to have one student explain something they have learned during that class period. When they have relayed the information correctly, call on another student to repeat what the first student said.

You can continue this review process by having another student repeat what the first two students said and explain an additional concept. You will notice students taking notes on what their fellow classmates have said!

Remember: Use time at the end of class to review that day's lesson.

Not all learning activities need to deal with the material you teach. Just like a muscle being exercised, there must be rest time in order for the brain to build strength. When the brain rests, it can be primed for future learning and for the assimilation of what you taught earlier in the class period. One way to enhance learning and efficiently fill the time left in class is to take what is often called "Breaks for the Brain." These strategies are structured and guided times for brain relaxation. These activities will depend on the age and level of instruction. Since the brain needs a rest in order to process the lesson's content, these are some possible "brain resting" activities:

- Breathing exercises. Guide your students in deep-breathing relaxation with relaxation music if possible.

- Gentle movements. Have your students stand and guide them into slow, steady motions. Incorporate breathing techniques as well. Keep it light if it is not a P.E. class!
- Simon Says game. Have the students stand and do a few minutes of Simon (or insert your name) Says, which involves body movements.

With these activities and the review practices mentioned above, you can use your remaining class time wisely when there's not enough time left to develop a new topic properly.

Remember: Develop strategies to use class time wisely.

Insight 11

Help Build a Better Brain through Repetition and Spacing

IN ORDER TO UNDERSTAND THE PROPER STRUCTURING OF LESSON PLANS and activities for your students, you must be aware of how their brains work and how learning is achieved. Our brain contains a multitude of web-like connections between neurons called synapses. These connections are complicated interactions that are reinforced by spaced stimuli and repetition. Spacing means that the information we're exposed to needs a time delay for restructuring neural networks. Spacing and repetition of information is the start of the formation of memories.

Because of spacing, learning literally changes the structure of the brain by strengthening synapses between neurons and by adding more synaptic connections. This process builds new proteins in the brain, which takes time.

Spacing of information allows for a more complete and longer-lasting ability to retrieve the information. New learning causes new synapses to form within memory areas, and spaced repetition stabilizes these synapses, moving the learning from short-term memory to long-term memory.

Allowing space between the introductions of new material enhances retention. Often teachers give an abundance of information in rapid succession without allowing space between concepts. Proper spacing allows downtime for brain neurons to replace and repair receptors in the synapse.

How do you achieve spacing? The answer depends on the level and difficulty of the material. When you introduce several difficult concepts, allow time between each of the concepts. By returning to the various learning styles, you can plan various hands-on kinesthetic reinforcements using coloring, model building, or games to strengthen and emphasize the material before moving on to new concepts.

Spacing and allowing time for review enhances the ability to recall the information from storage. Some teachers may highlight this process by using informal pre-testing, using some question-and-answer time at the introduction of a concept in order to "prime" the students' brains to accept the material more efficiently.

Remember: Allowing proper time between concepts taught will enhance memory and retrieval of information.

Research finds that the learning process can also be enhanced by emotional factors. Fear can "speed up" the process so that details of a frightening event can be recalled years later. The purpose of recalling a frightening event is for our own protection. Of course, this is *not* a technique that you should use in the classroom, but emotion can be harnessed in a positive way to enhance long-term recall. By adding applicable stories, games, and even humor into the information, you have created an emotional tag that helps in information recall.

Our knowledge of brain science is useful in planning the amount of material to teach, the number of repetitions to have, and the spacing of evaluations. The process of getting information into memory is encoding; storage is the retention of this information. Both encoding and storage are linked: Material is encoded and stored best if it is meaningful to the student. Connections can occur when material is related to other information, such as a personal story or even a mnemonic device.

The only way you know if the student is storing subject matter is from the retrieval of information. Recovery of learned material occurs best with frequent, small-sized evaluations rather than with fewer, large-quantity examinations.

Help Build a Better Brain through Repetition and Spacing

Some grade levels use songs to stimulate encoding as well as retrieval. Most kindergarten and first-grade students learn their ABCs by the Alphabet Song that most adults can still recite. Having your students create connections or devices to help remember the subject of a lesson is helpful in storing the information. You may have students take familiar songs and use grammar rules or math formulas for lyrics.

Remember: When students have ownership of their education, it will become more meaningful to them.

Information enters into short-term memory before it is stored in long-term memory. If too much information is encoded at the same time, a sort of neural traffic jam occurs. Memories need time to flow from short-term into long-term storage; therefore, proper spacing of material is as important as the amount of repetition for encoding into memory. Basically, the spacing and repetitive model of learning is like saying, "Don't eat the whole pizza in one bite. Divide it into smaller portions and eat frequently but with proper spacing!"

Expanding this analogy, we can make a mess of things if we try to eat the pizza, drink a soda, and FaceTime a friend all at the same moment. Multitasking does not aid in learning. You should make sure that distractions are at a minimum when you present a new concept. Students can't properly store information when they are expected to be doing several tasks at the same time or if there are other disruptions in the classroom.

Remember: Multitasking does not aid in learning.

Too much time between reviews and evaluations can be as harmful as too little time. Students often become frustrated when they return to your class and have forgotten some or all of the material from the previous class. Reassure them that this forgetfulness is normal since it is part of how their brains works. They must, however, revisit the material before the memory fades even more. (The next Insight explains how the forgetting of concepts has its place in learning.)

Insight 11

How much repetition students need will, of course, depend on the difficulty and level of the material you teach. You achieve repetition in many ways. You can conduct a series of open-ended questions that anyone can answer, or you can return to the popsicle jar and pull out names. Small group student-led reviews can work if you monitor their work closely. Of course, repetition is generally the backbone of homework assignments.

Remember: You need repetition when you want to strengthen memory and foster learning.

Insight 12

Forgetting Has Its Place in Learning

STUDENTS IN MIDDLE SCHOOL AND HIGH SCHOOL OFTEN QUOTE THIS poem:

The more you study—the more you know.

The more you know—the more you forget.

The more you forget—the less you know.

So why study?

Brain science doesn't totally agree with this sentiment, but the poem is not completely off-base. In reality, as the previous lesson pointed out, forgetting is actually a part of learning, since forgetting can strengthen cognitive retention as long as you revisit the material in a short period of time. With the proper spacing of information, allowing some time for the material to be forgotten can actually enhance recall.

So when do we study? One teacher jokingly told his students, "The state law that says you have to wait until the night before a test to study has been repealed!" As teachers we often encourage our students to study, but do we teach them how to study? As we have stated, one of the best ways to study is by frequently revisiting small amounts of material. This concept is behind one of your student's most dreaded activities: homework.

You need to analyze two factors: the type of homework you assign and the reason for giving the assignment. The purpose of homework is to offer review and reinforcement of the material. Homework is not assignments that load the student down with busy work to obtain more grades for student evaluation. Outside work should have the direct purpose of reviewing the material you taught, or in some cases, the first look at material that you will teach in the next class meeting.

When retrieval is high, as when we first learn something, repetition does very little to place this information into our long-term memory. But when we allow material to be "forgotten" and then revisited or "re-viewed," the information allows for better long-term memory storage. Of course, understand that in "forgetting," the information is not gone, only that recall is low.

How often have you looked up a phone number and dialed it, and five minutes later if someone asks you the number, you've totally forgotten it? Interestingly, most people can recall many years later their first childhood phone number and possibly the numbers of old friends. Why is that? Because you used those numbers often and had spacing between their usages. Eventually, the numbers were stored in your long-term memory.

Researchers believe that memories don't decay and cease to exist but are neural clusters that basically become inactive. The brain uses at least 25 percent of our total energy. In order to conserve this precious energy, our brains learn to forget, or place unuseful memories into a quiet state; therefore, forgetting is a natural state our brains use for energy conservation.

How does this information apply to our students' forgetting of the concepts we teach? The information that our brains turn off happens to be experiences that are not deemed important because the stimulus is a one-time event, such as looking up a phone number and using it once. But with repetition, the brain perceives the information as important and retrieval becomes easier. By experiencing and then forgetting and then experiencing a concept again, the dormant neurons are awakened and learning has occurred.

In the pattern of view–forget–review, material has an opportunity to connect with other memorized information in order to strengthen its retrieval. It's well-known that the brain will "prune" unused information;

however, the pruning occurs from retrievable memory, not necessarily from long-term memory storage. An experience or fact can be brought to the surface many years after you stored it, even if you think it's been forgotten; thus memory storage in a healthy brain is considered limitless. The problem comes with our finite ability to recall the stored information. In other words, all your stuff is still in a locked closet, and you just have to find the right key!

The spacing and reviewing enhances our ability to recall the information from storage. Some teachers begin this process by using informal pre-testing with some question-and-answer time at the introduction of a concept in order to prepare the students' brains to accept the material more efficiently.

When you introduce a new topic or concept, students can experience interference from their stored memory if the new material is very similar to recently learned information. If at all possible, try to organize your teaching syllabus so that similar topics are not taught in tandem. If impossible, you should point out the similarities and differences in the concepts to reduce interference.

Remember: Short-term forgetting can enhance long-term memory and recall.

Insight 13

Curiosity and Gap Instruction

RESEARCH SHOWS THAT STUDENTS REMEMBER INFORMATION BEST when they demonstrate a curiosity for the material. The brain responds to a desire to learn, stimulating the reward response that, in turn, increases LPT (long-term potentiation or long-term memory). Curiosity is a state of motivation in which the brain perceives what you teach as valuable to the students' future.

The question is this: How do teachers foster curiosity?

First, you must realize what you *can't* do. You can't raise interest by demand. Attempting to force curiosity simply creates disinterest or even boredom. You enhance inquisitiveness by presenting information with gaps. Create an environment where you ask questions and lead the students to the answers by offering enough information so that the students realize it's possible to discover the concept on their own. If they feel that they have no chance of understanding the lesson, curiosity will wane.

One strategy is the Socratic method, with modifications. This is a method where you ask a series of questions, questions designed to ultimately lead the students to an eventual conclusion. The questions must come from either material that you have covered or simply from the students' life experiences. In no way should the students feel pressured or anxious.

In this activity there are no wrong answers, just misguided responses, which you set straight at the end of the exercise as you review the ideas that the students discussed. If they don't perceive the exercise as an oral test, they'll feel safe; curiosity will be heightened and they will be more open to further experimentation. But you must lead them with small bits of information, questions, and comments. The questions need to be prepared ahead of time in order to guide the students toward a final concept. At the same time, you should allow for improvisation since you have no idea how they will answer.

Be sure to guide the discussion, always steering students back on task, because responses may move into uncharted territory. Without your proper guidance, students' may experience information overload and shut down. The shutdown is common after assignments such as "Read chapter 3 tonight." Chapter 3 may contain a great amount of material to digest, too much content to process at one time.

Instead, providing gaps in material allows students to discover the connections leading to quick rewards. The frequent reward system creates a learning incentive when the brain produces "feel-good" chemicals in a relatively short span of time. The outcome is a desire to continue learning. The long-term potentiation created is the difference between something memorized and something learned.

Remember: Don't simply tell, but allow for discovery.

If students can discover a concept, they're more likely to remember it and associate this knowledge with other experiences.

An example of a discovery exercise is when students study volume in science or math class. They are given a cylinder containing a premeasured amount of water (preferably colored), but no measurements are written on the container. Another differently shaped container also has the same amount of water, but students don't know that.

At this point, the teacher asks which container has the most water. This is the "gap" in information, regardless of their answer. Often they'll choose the container with the taller waterline; but whatever their choice, they'll make a discovery. Now is the time to allow them to discover. They pour the water from each container into a separate measured container, proving that both containers have the same volume of water.

What did they learn from this discovery activity? Many things, depending on what concepts you wish to reinforce. You now have their attention because you gave them ownership over their own education. This experience can now springboard into a discussion of volume and the mathematics involved, or it can simply demonstrate that things aren't always the way we see them.

The point is to use a gap to enhance the students' curiosity and experience so that they can discover the concepts you wish for them to learn. You begin by being more of a guide than someone who is simply tossing out facts. Sure, the facts need to come from the teacher and previous lessons and reading, but first, you prepare the mind by enhancing curiosity and then layer on more complex concepts.

Remember: Prepare the students' minds by allowing them to discover, make mistakes, retry, and succeed.

Insight 14

Teaching Machines versus Humans

What place does technology have in the classroom? This question is more pertinent today than it was a decade or more ago. When the pandemic hit in 2020, most schools across the country, as well as around the world, had to resort to online instruction. After many years of teaching, master teachers were forced to conduct classes on the computer. Teaching almost any subject or grade level via computer was challenging, to say the least. During this trying time in our nation, all teachers learned the benefits as well as the limitations of online instruction.

Because of the pandemic, technology has become a necessity in continuing instruction from home. The question now has changed. We no longer ask if technology should be in the classroom, but rather, what role it should play. Tech is here to stay. The answer to this question will, of course, depend on the subject, level of instruction, and age group you teach.

Technology has changed the traditional classroom. One thing is for sure: Anytime a politician uses education as his platform, you can bet that the next words you hear are, "laptops and tablets in the classroom and more testing," a double-edged sword that depends on the implementation of technology.

Research finds that, because of the extreme degree of information and communication technologies that enter into our daily lives, these technologies are increasing and are widely adopted in the classroom setting. Classrooms where these technologies are implemented demonstrate a mixed impact on student performance and achievement.

Some research indicates that the use of laptops and tablets in class may encourage students to procrastinate. The temptation to look at other material on the screen exists, making it much more difficult for the teacher to monitor each student's computer and reducing the efficiency of the time the students spend in class. While computers have the ability to multitask, our brains can't effectively operate this way.

Multitasking can have a negative impact on memorization. Even though students who multitask using a computer device can actually complete more tasks, they tend not to do the task as well as students who multitask with paper and pencil.

Remember: Multitasking decreases student comprehension, especially if the tasks are performed on a tablet or laptop.

Another area of research is note-taking on a computer versus the old-fashioned handwritten notes. The computer allows for faster note-taking, which can be a positive thing. Yet handwriting, since it's slower, allows for more effective mental processing of the material, thus activating kinesthetic brain activity. Writing also allows the freedom of creating diagrams and even doodling as needed to reinforce the notes. The use of a laptop to take notes has been shown to decrease comprehension as compared to handwritten notetaking.

Remember: Handwritten notetaking is superior to laptop notation.

Computer technology has had a positive impact on the classroom teacher in the way of communication between the teacher and the students' parents. Most school districts require their teachers to keep up-to-date web pages for both students and parents to see upcoming assignments and announcements from the classroom.

Also, because of the computer, teachers can have a direct and immediate connection to administration and guidance as well as school resource officers and medical personnel.

Computers have opened up new possibilities for the classroom that were previously unavailable. Students have the ability to watch scientific or world events occurring in real time. The computer can bring the world closer to students by allowing them to connect with other classrooms across the globe, which is especially helpful in foreign language classes.

Also, professionals in particular fields can be brought into the classroom though online interviews or, at the very least, email. Before the computer these connections had to take place through mail, a slow process at best.

Most—if not all—teachers, especially in secondary education and beyond, require assignments to be completed and sent electronically. You need to remember that all of these tools are helpful and vital for instruction. But they're just that—tools. You need a hammer to build a house, but the hammer doesn't do the job alone. It needs to be in the hands of a skilled carpenter.

Some educational philosophies support the concept of a well-constructed algorithm that would remove most of the instruction from a teacher's hands. Many computer programs are wonderful tools for reinforcing what you have taught in the classroom setting, but they will never replace the one-on-one relationship of teacher and student.

New teachers coming into the profession are hopefully quite adept in the technology used for class instruction; however, technology does not prepare them for the skills they need to engage their students. All teachers should carve out some time in each class to teach without technology by using storytelling, class discussions, diagrams, role-playing, etc. Screen time has its place, but direct teacher-to-student instruction always proves effective.

The challenge facing today's teachers is how to balance technological information with traditional teacher-led instruction. They both play an important role in the classroom. With technology becoming more affordable for school districts, and new educational software being developed each day, computer instruction is becoming more prevalent in today's classrooms.

Remember: The best educational strategy is always human to human.

Insight 15

Journaling Has Its Place in Any Subject

With the development of writing skills, students have acquired a valuable tool to enhance learning and retention. Even if they have not developed proper sentence structure skills, journaling can be used in every subject matter and at every level. Journal drawing can be a wonderful form of communication. By journaling after each lesson, activity, game, or lab exercise, students will take personal ownership of the experience. The number one rule of journaling is that there are no rules. The activity must remain open-ended.

Teachers often use reflective journaling, a guided exercise in which you give the students some writing prompts, yet still leave room for open-ended creativity. Some idea prompts for reflective journaling may include the following:

- Briefly describe the activity.
- Who was involved in the activity?
- What part did you have in the activity?
- What are your feelings about what happened in the activity?

Journaling is not a time for students simply to spit back the concepts presented to them and try to impress the teacher. Instead, it's a time for them to express their feelings about the activity or lesson. This opportunity gives each student a time to develop his own voice.

Insight 15

In a journaling activity, failure isn't an option; therefore, the stress of not doing it correctly is gone, and students are free to express themselves by allowing their brains to process the information from an emotional perspective, placing the information and concepts into long-term memory.

Educational research shows us that emotions modify every part of cognitive development. When students learn something new, the emotional and cognitive areas of their brains become interrelated, especially if the emotion is a positive one, opening paths for new learning and providing motivation.

Remember: Journaling inspires creativity, which leads to learning.

One important idea concerning journaling is that the activity should be completed using paper and pen or pencil. It is not an exercise for the keyboard because the students' brains are more active when they write by hand than when they type on the keyboard. Sensorimotor parts of the brain are activated, allowing the memory portions of their brains to work more efficiently.

For older students, handwriting improves reading by connecting to reading circuits in the brain. Writing skills also improve. Additionally, handwriting can act as a type of mediation, allowing the students to concentrate on the moment, thereby lowering stress levels and anxiety.

Remember: Journaling needs to be a handwritten activity.

Journaling for young students who are learning to read is important. Obviously, this activity should be more guided since their sentence structure abilities are just developing. Handwritten letters are processed in a different area of the brain than handwritten words, and with practice, these regions communicate, improving reading and writing skills.

As the instructor, the nuts and bolts of this activity are up to you. One possibility is to keep the student journals and hand them out at the end of an activity or class. Make it clear that you're not grading them on content, but it is a required assignment where they are to address the prompts that you have given them. Students will be more honest in their responses if they know that no one else besides you will ever read their words.

When you look at the journals, simply use a check, smiley face, or some nonjudgmental mark so that they know you have read their entries. Of course, there are going to be students who resist and only write a few words and then become a distraction to the rest of the class. But if you make this a "quiet time of reflection," they may eventually come around to enjoying this exercise.

Remember: Positive emotions lead to motivation, which has a strong influence on reasoning and long-term memory.

Insight 16

Front Door–Back Door

Most frustrated parents have answered the constant question posed by their kids on a road trip: "How much farther?"

The parents assure the children that they will arrive at their destination sometime in the near future. Somewhat satisfied, the kids settle back into coloring books or iPads.

The concept is much the same in the classroom. In beginning a new lesson, it helps for you to use what is commonly called "front door–back door," usually called instructional objectives. These are goals for the students, referred to as learning or behavioral objectives.

You can introduce the basic framework of a lesson by explaining how much material you will cover during the class period, and then continue to fill in the details. Depending on the level of instruction, you can present an outline or some statements about where this material is going and when it will be finished.

Presenting clear objectives should be done on a daily basis so students will know what you expect of them for that class period and for the entire unit of study. When students have a basic understanding of what you expect and how much material you will present, they can free up some working memory (aka, short-term memory) and learn more efficiently.

Instructional objectives should be short and measurable statements that let students know what you expect them to learn and how you will evaluate the material. Objectives need to be specific, using action verbs such as *list, complete, identify, design,* and *calculate*. Avoid vague and immeasurable terminology such as *understand, know, learn,* and *appreciate*.

Remember: When you write instructional objectives, make them specific, measurable, and relevant to the material being taught.

Objectives not only help the student but they help you as well. You create them as a guide for their lesson plans. They are the foundation for the material you cover by determining the scope and depth of the lesson. When you create your instructional objectives for a unit of study, you are designing the framework from which students will build on. This truly gives you a "front door–back door" to instruction.

Once the objectives have been stated verbally or posted, your instructional methods need to be correlated to these objectives. Using graphic organizers or concept maps that use visual symbols to indicate concepts is helpful. Graphic organizers have proven effective, especially with students who have difficulty paying attention or reading an outline. Otherwise, a basic outline, in the form of a handout or bulleted statements on a whiteboard, chalkboard, or PowerPoint slide, is a great help in keeping students on track.

Outlines help students in many ways. First, they show the boundaries of the lesson. When you present the scope of the material and explain it from a big-picture perspective, your pupils are more likely to make connections and discover where the details are placed along the framework. When you teach a class of older students, the outline should in no way be substituted for classroom notes since some students, not unlike water running downhill, are going to take the easiest route and avoid notetaking.

Second, the outline approach helps keep the students on track as you explain the material, and gives you an opportunity to refer to terms and definitions listed in the outline, thus reinforcing the concepts. The outline will allow the students to know how much material they're expected to learn, freeing their minds from wondering, *How much farther?*

Remember: By establishing the border of a puzzle first, you can more clearly see where the other pieces fit.

Insight 17

Peer Learning

Each One, Teach One

You may have had the misfortune of sitting in a college class when another student asked the instructor a question, only to groan when the professor's response further confused the student asking the question. You might think, *I understand why he's confused. I can explain this better than the professor.* However, you don't necessarily know more than the professor—far from it—but as a teacher-in-training, you simply understood the other student's question and knew how to explain the concept on a different level.

Using students' natural inclination for social exchanges, and the fact that one of the best ways to learn a subject is by teaching it to someone, have students teach concepts to each other. In small groups they tend to understand quickly why their classmates are having difficulty learning the material.

Often, a teacher may be too far removed from the fundamentals that trip up a student in the early stages of learning a concept and neglect some basics that the students need to understand the concept. Other students in the group may understand and be able to plug in information needed to complete the picture.

Remember: One of the best ways for students to learn a subject is to teach the content to someone.

In a small group setting, students feel more comfortable admitting that they aren't grasping a concept and asking the teacher to explain the ideas more. At this point, you can focus your instruction on a few students, being much more efficient in your teaching and in helping them understand. You should be certain, though, that each student contributes equally to the group. If not, intervene and guide the group participants so that everyone is involved.

Remember: Each student in a group should participate equally in a group learning exercise.

Cooperative learning can be an excellent strategy, or it can blow up in your face if not handled correctly. It is your goal for the students to work together, reinforcing the concepts; however, without proper monitoring, the opposite can happen. You must control any possible disruptions and provide the proper atmosphere for learning.

The physical arrangement of the classroom can help or hurt cooperative learning. Depending on the school facility, group arrangement may be a challenge. Some degree of an open-floor plan will allow you easy access to all the groups, giving you the ability to monitor activity. The main challenge for you is to think through the layout of the classroom in advance so that the structure is conducive to learning and is not a matter of distraction. It is important for the position and organization of the classroom to have proper flow so you can have quick access to every group and can monitor progress as well as get ahead of any possible disruptions.

Remember: The arrangement of your classroom should allow access to every student.

The very last thing that you need to do is to use this activity time to sit at your desk and grade papers or complete some other classroom task, leaving the students to their own devices. Constant monitoring of the study groups to check for misunderstandings and to evaluate the accuracy of students' relaying the material to their peers will allow students the opportunity to ask you questions as they arise and for you to keep all groups on task.

Remember: If learning is driven by the inquisitive mind of a student, that learning must be met with an equally creative mind of a teacher.

A student wanting to ask a question can feel threatened or intimidated in a large class environment; in a small group setting, though, students are much more likely to ask questions once they discover their classmates may have the same misconceptions about the material. Students fear asking a "dumb question," which is compounded when a larger number of peers are listening.

Remember: The only dumb questions are the ones that were never asked.

The cooperative learning approach not only allows students to explore and discover concepts in their own way, it can also be useful in your uncovering misguided ideas that students may have learned years earlier. Not only are these groups an excellent instructional strategy when organized properly, but they can also result in a fact-finding mission for the teacher. If a misconception about the material seems to be prevalent among several groups, the best strategy would be to get the whole class's attention and correct the error, and then allow the cooperative groups to continue.

Insight 18
Teacher-Centered versus Student-Centered

IN EDUCATIONAL PHILOSOPHY WE OFTEN HEAR THE TERMS *student-centered* educational theory and *teacher-centered approach*. Traditionally, in the United States, education has used a teacher-centered approach: The teacher teaches and the students listen and hopefully learn the material.

In the old-school method of a teacher-centered class, there is rote memorization of facts, and the textbook is the guide with information that is possibly, and almost certainly, outdated. In this teacher-centered class, priority is given to grades and rank, not the learners.

The teacher-centered method is still in use but it has been updated. In the more modern teacher-centered approach the teacher imparts the information and the students take notes and listen. This approach deviates slightly from the old-school method because it's not totally lecture-driven, since it involves other activities that are still teacher-driven in scope.

Many administrators prefer to lean toward a teacher-centered approach because it creates order and the teacher is in complete control. There are students who learn best in a controlled environment, but there are those who get bored and their minds wander.

In a student-centered classroom, the students discover the concepts through various activities and play. Obviously, you design the activities, but the students work through them at their own paces. You act like more of a facilitator who gives guidance and feedback. Cooperative learning, as mentioned in the last insight, becomes an important facet in this approach.

Students crave stimulation and learning occurs when the brain is stimulated. In the student-centered classroom, play is important, but you can't always distinguish between learning and playing. Each step in the play process has a purpose and occurs in sequential order to ultimately achieve the end goal of understanding a concept. Students work at their own individual paces or in a cooperative group, but the classroom can become chaotic and distracting to some students.

If a school wishes to appear progressive in its educational approach, it will usually describe its curriculum as student-centered, but this is not necessarily the best option. Many student-centered programs are geared toward older students. They are more project-based and often involve internships where students work in the community beside professionals in a field.

Today, educators lean toward a balanced classroom concept, which is a combination of the two approaches.

In this combination approach, the traditional teacher-centered method is combined with student-centered activities. Often current events and social circumstances can be a springboard to discussion and playful activities. You need to allow students to question and learn, not simply accept a set of facts. Student-centered activities strengthen the psychological aspects of a student's learning.

Also, in this approach, the teacher-centered portion of a lesson comes from your supplying information and then leading the students in a student-centered discovery activity. At some point, this can lead to an evaluation because testing in various forms is necessary.

Another approach uses the term *hybrid* method, a blend of classroom learning and eLearning where students have a choice of traditional and online classes. The hybrid approach involves unique scheduling and requires a special curriculum.

Of course, we want our students to love to learn and interact with others, but in the real world of education, we must evaluate their progress and measure it against standards. We have to balance the idea that learning can be fun with the very real fact that learning can also be hard work.

There are concepts that must be mastered, but hopefully the mastery can be enjoyable as well.

Remember: Students can be beautifully well-adjusted, but eventually we are all accountable for the material we have learned in order to be successful in future endeavors.

Insight 19

Use Your Teaching Energy Wisely and Stay Healthy

SADLY, TOO OFTEN WE SPEND MUCH OF OUR TIME AND ENERGY DESIGNing an activity, or even an entire curriculum, around the lazy or behaviorally-challenged students. Depending on the academic level you're teaching, a percentage of students will choose to be difficult and not follow directions; therefore, you must prepare for this inevitability in your daily lesson plan structure as well as in the creation of tests, activities, and worksheets. Unfortunately, it's impossible to foreshadow every situation.

Since it takes a lot of teaching experience to be able to predict the uncooperative mind of some students, concentrate your energy on reaching the mind of the students who are interested in learning. Obviously, you want to engage all students, but you need to conserve most of your teaching energy and apply it toward the receptive students; otherwise, you will simply be chasing problems all day and not connecting with the students who do wish to learn.

Of course, you can't disregard the less-then-receptive students. There are many strategies for engaging them. You aren't calling their names for correction; instead, you are engaging them in the lesson. And be sure to call the names of interested students as well. One of the simplest strategies is to call them by name in the course of presenting information. Any time you can prevent or correct a situation and still conserve your teaching energy is an advantage to both you and your students.

Remember: It takes precious time and energy to anticipate most classroom problems. Spend your teaching energy wisely.

As a teacher, you can easily become overwhelmed, even on the best teaching days. This downward emotional spiral can creep up on you and worsens when you feel that your students haven't learned anything. There will be days when you feel as though your students would have learned just as much if you had stayed home and had never gotten out of bed. As tempting as that may be, you know that you have to try your best to reach your students—all of them. You can focus on the receptive students but you also need to understand why the less receptive students are behaving in that manner.

Remember: You impact students positively or negatively every single day.

In order to be ready for the task of teaching, it is paramount that you conserve your mental, physical, and emotional energies. Remember that the way you structure your lessons can either create or diminish behavior problems.

Remember: You must anticipate good days and good outcomes, rather than the opposite.

One overlooked area of energy conservation is how you spend your personal time. Teaching is a profession in which, even if you're not physically in the classroom, you're always involved with some aspect of teaching: grading papers; designing activities; reading and responding to student, parent, or administrative emails; and of course, studying to stay current with the subject you teach.

Since you're a teacher, you'll find lessons for your students in every aspect of your life—in a novel you're reading or a movie you're watching, or while digging in the garden or simply going for a walk; something will stimulate an idea for a lesson. The stimulation is good and makes for excellent teaching opportunities, but you need balance. When the creative juices flow, embrace them but know that you must control them. As a teacher, it's difficult to be "off work."

Remember: Teacher preparation takes energy. Schedule "downtime" to recharge.

Some of the best teachers can experience burnout simply by not scheduling time for themselves. Classroom preparation is not the only area that requires your time and energy. If you're not careful, you can take on more responsibility at school than you can handle. All schools require a degree of duties and committee participation from each teacher, a necessary and expected part of the job. Administrators know who the responsible faculty members are, and often they'll load them up with extra activities and duties, simply because they know the jobs will be done well.

A new teacher may find this attention flattering and try to prove that they are a vital part of the school by taking on too many tasks. The upside is that you will most likely become an important asset to the school faculty, a positive place to be in by helping the school and your students, and for job security (if for no other reason than you're willing to take on tasks that no one else wants). If you're not careful, however, you can inflate your importance to the school and allow yourself to become overloaded with responsibilities.

Remember: If you're not in your classroom tomorrow, someone else will be. No teacher is indispensable.

Now add to your school commitments the community—including church and civic organizations—which teachers seem to gravitate toward due to their volunteer spirit. You realize that your place in the community is an important part of being a teacher. When your students see you giving your time, it's a wonderful influence, but it's easy to take on more responsibilities than you're capable of performing efficiently.

Most teachers are schedulers and organizers by trade and habit. Use these skills to your advantage. You must plan, schedule, and adhere to downtime as rigorously as your teaching preparation time. Your mental and physical health may suffer from too much added responsibility, hurting you and being unfair to your family.

Remember: You are replaceable at work, but not at home.

A good teacher plans a lesson where students are on task throughout the class period, a mindset that will creep into your home life. Even during planned downtime, you may feel as if you need to be accomplishing something by constantly being on task. Find some time to just "be." Everything doesn't have to be an accomplishment.

Remember: Doing nothing is doing something. A teacher must work at not burning the proverbial candle at both ends.

Being a teacher doesn't mean that you have license to ignore your physical health or mental well-being. Teaching is a rewarding profession, and most of the time there is joy in being an educator, but it can be a horrible experience if you are teaching while you're sick. Trying to keep a high level of energy in front of your students while fighting a fever or some other physical malady is nearly impossible. Every teacher, especially new teachers, will catch colds or viruses, whatever the students bring into your classroom. After all, the classroom is a haven for germs, with many students invading your personal space and bringing a multitude of germs with them.

Remember: You must show up for *you* before you can show up for others.

Your voice and your stamina are two physical properties that you use every teaching day, so it is imperative that you protect yourself from illness and injury. Of course, all school districts have sick leave days, but preparing for a substitute teacher is oftentimes more work than teaching the class yourself. For that reason many teachers will work while sick (not a good idea) to avoid the stress of extra preparation.

Use Your Teaching Energy Wisely and Stay Healthy

As an intelligent adult, you should know how to take care of yourself, but here are a few reminders about being at the top of your game physically and mentally:

- Be sure to schedule an annual checkup with a doctor and follow their directions.
- Get moving! Yes, teaching can be exhausting, but you must add proper physical exercise to your already busy week.
- Eat right. After a stressful day at school, it is very tempting to grab some fast food. Cooking takes time but it is worth it if you eat nutritious meals. Not only will you have more energy, but your immune system will be in better shape to ward off all the germs you are exposed to in the classroom.
- Develop a balanced social life with people who encourage and inspire you. Too, we all need some "me" time, but too much of just "you" can be harmful mentally as well as physically. Don't confuse isolation with solitude.
- Work in some stress relief activities such as a walk in nature, a yoga class, a relaxing massage, or quiet time on your porch with a cup of tea while listening to the birds sing.
- Get proper sleep. Brain science constantly reveals the benefits of good sleep. Try to get seven to eight hours of sleep every night. Don't rely on the weekend to catch up on sleep. Burning the midnight oil to grade papers or create lesson plans will eventually degrade your health and well-being. Don't drink alcohol or caffeine near bedtime. Turn off screens and have a routine before bed that tells your brain you are ready for sleep. During your waking hours, your brain is not able to remove all the metabolic waste that it has gathered because it is too busy with other important processes. It is only during sleep that we "take out the trash." If you want to stay sharp for your students and family and be able to experience a long teaching career, then make sleep a priority.
- Don't smoke, or stop if you do. You know better.

Your career as a teacher can be overwhelming at times. There is probably not a teacher alive who, at some point in her career, hasn't fantasized about running off to a mountain cabin or shack on the beach and forgetting about it all, a normal reaction to stress. But if you want to minimize these thoughts, protect your energy in the classroom and your physical and mental health and you will experience a long, rewarding career. See Insight 28: *Teacher Burnout and Rewiring Your Brain*.

Remember: Guard your energy and take care of your mind and body. You only have one of each.

Insight 20

Redirection versus Rejection

No matter the age of the students, they have lives outside the classroom. Certain students constantly want to share their experiences with the class, even when they are not directly relevant to the topic of the lesson. A discussion in biology about cell division might spur a student to ask questions about his grandmother's cancer diagnosis.

A story about a dog may open the floodgate of personal experiences with pets. You should view any question as an opportunity to make the subject relevant to the students, rather than rejecting it as a class interruption. A short discussion related to the comments or questions can pique interest, and then you can skillfully return to the topic you're discussing.

Brain research shows us that the same areas of the brain that register physical pain also register social pain. Even though emotional pain is not processed in exactly the same manner as physical pain, the rejection still hurts. An apparent threat stimulates our fight-or-flight response in the brain. In just a few seconds a student may lash out at you, depending on the level of rejection and/or the emotional state of the student. This situation places you in a position where some disciplinary action may be necessary.

However, most of the time the student will respond with a flight rather than a fight response; he may turn inward and not ask any more questions. Since humans are programmed to avoid pain whenever possible, he will avoid speaking out in the future if he feels rejected, thereby avoiding the pain. To the student, the rejection is a perceived threat.

Insight 20

Sometimes we feel pain or uncomfortable feelings simply by association. If you observe someone cutting his finger, you may wince in pain, even though you were not cut. A student will identify with a teacher's rejection of another student just as if he were rejected.

Remember: Be careful how you speak to a student. Others are watching.

Some students may be extra sensitive to rejection by an authority. Maybe parents or older siblings do not take them seriously at home. Possibly a previous teacher responded negatively to their questions. These students will most likely interpret the teacher's rejection in a very personal way, since rejection for them is being told they are not wanted or are not worthy.

In any case, from the student's perspective, he is taking a risk asking a question in class. How you respond to the question may determine how receptive the student is to learning the material.

Knowing that redirecting off-topic responses can be a fine line to maneuver since a cascade of personal stories may flow through the class, you must never come across as rejecting any student's comments, or any interest in the topic that's been forged may quickly dissipate. If a student's question or comment seems inappropriate, it's vital to determine whether the statement is sincere and not simply a ploy to disrupt the classroom. Many of your students won't always have verbal abilities or proper vocabulary to express themselves without sounding crude. A gentle correction will at these times be useful without demeaning or embarrassing the student.

Remember: Not all students know how to ask a question properly.

Oftentimes, an off-topic question can be an opportunity for learning. Allowing a controlled tangent can blossom into a valuable discussion, a teachable moment discussed in an earlier insight.

By building on the question at hand and redirecting to the subject matter, you have created a mental hook for the students to better retrieve

Redirection versus Rejection

the information. Also, you have nurtured student self-confidence by creating a feeling that they have contributed to the class discussion, even after you've carefully returned to the original topic.

Once you have handled the situation properly, the student will feel accepted and safe in asking future questions. Your teacher flexibility becomes very important here. If you see the tangent for what it really is—a student eager to add to the discussion—then you can carefully identify the relevant parts of the comment and redirect, rather than reject.

Remember: Redirection is always a better option than rejection.

Insight 21

Develop More Than One Passion

There is an old, outdated adage that says "There are three reasons to go into teaching as a career—June, July, and August." This statement implies that teachers teach because of the time they are *not* teaching. This assertion is loaded with negativity. From this assertion one might gather that teachers simply teach for the money, not for the love of their craft. First, the adage is totally inaccurate in today's educational system: With creative school calendars, it's rare to find a school system that allows three entire months off from the classroom. (And anyone who thinks teachers go into the profession for the money has never seen a teacher's paycheck!) Enough said.

Another saying that boils a teacher's blood is "People who can't do, teach." You don't have to walk down the halls of any public or private school to find men and women who are professionals in their respective fields. The saying fails to address the passion teachers develop for their craft.

Effective teachers have a passion for what they teach. You not only develop a love for the craft and art of teaching but you cultivate a passion for your subject. Many even say teaching is a calling. Elementary teachers are unique because they usually teach a wide range of subjects, but many elementary schools have adopted more of a secondary approach with teachers who specialize in a particular subject and students who go to their class for instruction. Overall, elementary teachers have the ability to develop multiple passions.

Regardless of their curriculum, most secondary teachers have a passion for at least one subject. Because of this developed passion, most teachers will spend many hours learning their subject matter, either by taking extracurricular classes or reading on their own, creating an effective, knowledgeable teacher who is skilled in her subject area.

Extracurricular activities play a very real part in any teacher's school life. Everyone will either choose or be assigned an activity or club to sponsor. If the administration gives them the opportunity to choose, teachers often stay within their areas of expertise. A science teacher might become the advisor of the science club while an English teacher heads up a book club. A physical education teacher may coach soccer while a music teacher will direct an afterschool ensemble. Working in our area of knowledge is a comfortable place to be, but you never grow until you step out of your comfort zone.

Having an expert to lead a school organization that fits their skill set and abilities is a wonderful experience for the students and usually for the teacher as well, but teachers often need a break from the areas where they feel the most proficient. Because a teacher has an innate desire to learn, they often have multiple skills and they need to exercise these skills.

Occasionally, teachers should seek to be involved in areas dissimilar to their fields of study, challenging them to learn new skills or implement skills that have become dormant. Therefore, the abilities a teacher already possesses have a chance to rest and recharge. Not being in charge of an activity relieves some of the stress or effort spent organizing. You can learn new things and possibly develop new passions.

Brain science tells us that by trying different activities, new pathways develop and new connections are made between brain cells; these new connections allow you to mentally process faster and see patterns more efficiently. A novel activity recruits new brain circuits, which is good for your long-term brain health.

Another advantage of trying new things outside your comfort zone is the camaraderie with teachers who do not normally cross your path on a daily basis. These are people you see in a weekly teachers' meeting or sit next to in an occasional parent conference; but other than exchanging polite pleasantries, you don't know these teachers. Professional colleagues from other subject areas may offer you a different view of teaching strategies and classroom management that you otherwise would not encounter. By stepping out of your normal circle of teachers you not only share new educational ideas with fellow coworkers but you make good friends as well.

Remember: Stepping out of your comfort zone can improve your brain health, teaching skills, and mental health.

Insight 22

Stay Current

IN THE PAST, PEOPLE DID NOT CONSIDER TEACHING A PROFESSION AS much as a secondary job that was often held by a woman. Today, in most modern societies' views, teaching is a worthy profession and teachers are professionals. However, because salaries have not caught up with other professions that require an equal amount of education, some people may still consider teaching an ancillary profession. It is not. You are a professional, and like all professionals, you must stay current, not only with your subject matter or grade-level material but with research, policies, and modalities—the whole of educational information.

Two questions arise: Why and how?

First, let's address why a teacher must continue to seek out new teaching strategies.

As a teacher you should not expect to teach the same material the same way year after year. Research into brain science and how people learn is moving at lightning speed, telling us how the brain receives, processes, and retains information and the differences between individuals. Since not everyone absorbs packages of information in the same manner, you must alter teaching styles to accommodate these differences. As your experience builds, you will become aware of those practices that are working and those that are unsuccessful.

Remember: As a teacher, you must constantly be learning the newest methods in your craft.

How do you keep abreast of teachings' newest methods? All college students today are aware of a plethora of information online; students can obtain degrees and certifications without leaving the comfort of their home. Online courses offer a flexible way to be involved in a self-paced curriculum that fits your personal lifestyle.

Online educational literature from reputable sources is an excellent way to obtain practical information about teaching methods in any subject. Also, there is an abundance of online teacher forums where ideas and strategies are shared with other teaching professionals.

When you are deciding if an online versus an in-person course is better for you, be honest with yourself about how you learn. You should be taking the class to improve your teaching skills and knowledge, not just to renew your certificate. Are you a focused learner or do you tend to procrastinate? The answer should let you know which type of class you should enroll in.

Be sure to approach the online medium with caution. As wonderful a source as this may be, online can also be a harbor for misinformation and misguidance. It is best to get referrals from other teachers or district personnel before venturing into an online class.

Remember: When considering an online course, study the syllabus. If doesn't feel right, it probably isn't. Leave it alone.

Many teachers attend conferences and seminars where teachers engage in discussions face-to-face and get suggestions from other teachers about handling classroom situations and share teaching strategies. These activities are a wonderful way to network with fellow educators from different schools and districts and share information. It is a great idea to combine professional development classes with your required continuing education needs for updating your professional certificate. These classes may also be used to get credit for advanced degrees.

Always check with your state department of education if you plan to use a continuing education course for recertification.

One of the best ways to improve your teaching skills is to share strategies with a mentor. This relationship is most valuable if the mentor is in the same school and teaches the same grade level or subject matter. Too, many teaching strategies are universal and you can adapt them across the curriculum and grade levels. Before you realize it, a new teacher will seek you out as a mentor, a relationship that can be just as important to you as it is to the new teacher.

Keeping up with new technology, attending conferences, and developing lesson plans that are always fluid as well as managing a classroom can be very stressful. Don't add too many layers of stress to an already demanding work schedule. Staying current as a teacher is vital, but spread out your professional development so that it is not only manageable but enjoyable.

Remember: Staying current is essential, but be mindful of the added time and stress.

Insight 23
Classroom Organization and Displays

It's summertime and the new teacher walks into her classroom for the first time. This room is where she will be spending much of her waking moments, educating young minds and preparing them for their futures. Excitement builds as she looks at the blank walls and empty shelves and imagines how she can make the room more inviting. She experiments with different desk arrangements and floor plans, searching for the best configuration for both teaching and learning. It is now time to make this a refuge for knowledge. She needs to consider several factors when she plans her classroom décor and structure.

You should use the organization of your classrooms as a major part of your teaching plan. Classroom walls should be warm, and they should invite learning, but they should not be overcrowded. How to decorate your classroom will depend primarily on the grade level you teach. Elementary aged children have a harder time with selective focus, and they have a poorer ability to inhibit distractions than older, high school aged students.

Be careful not to bombard students with an excess of visual information since cognitive performance can be negatively affected by too much visual stimulation. Overdone classroom walls can lower student performance, but if properly balanced, wall art and other displays can be a benefit, assuming the material is relevant and engaging and not a distraction.

Here are some general rules to follow when arranging your classroom and decorating your walls:

- Avoid clutter. This rule is not just for the walls. Corners of the room are not storage areas unless items are neatly arranged, and that is only when your storage is limited. Clutter lowers valuable square footage needed for teaching and learning.
- Have inspiring role models and quotes portrayed on the walls, especially for older students.
- Keep at least 20 percent of the wall free with space between displays. Many students are very susceptible to overstimulation. Be aware of the quantity of bright-colored posters, which can be a distraction.

Remember: Swap wall displays often rather than adding more to an existing display.

- Increase natural light if at all possible. You obviously have no control over the number and size of windows, but attempt not to obstruct the ones that you have.
- Avoid controversial images and topics such as religion and politics unless your administration approves and your state teaching standards support them.

Remember: You are there to teach, not preach.

- Display student work when appropriate, but do not display grades. Exhibitions may be in the form of assigned projects or art work. If you display student work, give all students an equal opportunity to have their work shown.
- It is of the utmost importance to consider student safety when decorating your classroom. Be sure to keep any breakable materials such as glass vases, jars, terrariums, or lab equipment out of student reach. When you bring live material like flowers into the classroom, avoid any plants that have allergens or are poisonous. If you are not sure, consult your county's agricultural extension office. Avoid harmful animals that may bite or sting.

One important aspect of classroom décor is the physical arrangement of the furniture.

How to organize your classroom will depend on the age level and subject you are teaching. If other teachers will be using the same classroom, you will need to consider their needs as well as yours. If you have your own classroom, make it as open and inviting as possible.

The arrangement of the room should be designed so that desks are not facing outside distractions such as a playground or a busy road. Moreover, organize your room to provide you with easy access to every student. Another idea is to create an independent study area for a student to work by himself when the need arises.

If more furniture is needed for your classroom, ask fellow teachers if they have anything they are not using or consult with the school custodian about any unused pieces that might be sitting in storage. If need be, scour your local thrift shops for cheap, sturdy tables and chairs.

Remember: The proper arrangement of your classroom environment can make it a place for optimal learning and a sanctuary of joy to practice your craft.

INSIGHT 24

Professionalism

A PROFESSION IS AN OCCUPATION THAT REQUIRES EXTENSIVE AND RIGorous training and specific qualifications to meet a standard. Generally speaking, having a profession simply means you get paid to do the work. Teaching is a profession, but what does it mean to be a professional? Most teacher training courses would tell the aspiring teacher to display the knowledge and skills of a professional, but ironically, a universal definition of a professional does not exist. One reason is because many of the expectations of a professional educator depend upon your local community.

The following expectations of teacher professionalism can be considered universal, even though the particulars can change between school districts:

- Teachers are to maintain appropriate relations with students, parents, and fellow teachers. You should aim to treat all students equally. In reality, you might interact with some students more than others, simply because they are friends of your own children or you are acquainted with their parents outside the school environment. However, in the classroom and school setting, all students are to have the same opportunities. Never ever give the appearance of showing favoritism to any student.

- Don't put them on a friendly level with you. They are not your friends. They are not your peers. They are your students.

- Be careful about touching your students, even on their arms and shoulders. If you must touch a student due to a health or safety situation, always have another professional present.
- Many school districts have a strict code of conduct in relation to dress, hygiene, and grooming. Take pride in your appearance and dress in neat, clean clothes, and in styles and colors that are not distracting. You are in the classroom to educate, not to impress students with your sense of style and fashion.

Remember: Students don't want you to dress like them. They respect adults who dress like adults.

- School rules and procedures are to be followed. We cannot expect students to follow school mandates if we do not honor them as well. There may be times and particular circumstances when a school rule needs to be altered, and you should discuss any changes of school policy with administration, not the students. However, in emergency situations when you must consider the safety of a student, you may have to make a quick decision to suspend a rule.
- There should be promptness in work and assignments. Get to your classroom early and be ready to start class on time. You set a poor example when you require your students to be in class on time but are not ready to begin class yourself. Be prompt at turning in required paperwork to the administration as well as following up with parent contact.

Remember: We expect our students to be on time to class as well as with assignments. We should model this behavior.

- A teacher's conduct in the community should be above reproach, a standard that is especially true if you live in the community where you teach. Be very aware of the social mores and behavioral expectations of your community.

Your professionalism should be obvious in any social media presence you display. Administrators encourage class web pages where teachers can post assignments and class notifications for parents and students. Private email within these web pages can keep individuals current with classroom activities, especially in the case of extended absences. Also, remember that in correspondences, you need to use proper grammar. Avoid the use of popular online abbreviations. Keep the communication on-topic and away from personal discussions.

- Social media applications can be an excellent tool for contact with students and parents, but with your personal accounts, limitations to student access should be considered.

Remember: People are always watching. Teachers should have and practice a high standard of conduct.

- You should see that *all* students receive an equal chance to succeed. It goes without saying that some students are going to excel more than others; however, no teacher should give one student a greater opportunity to succeed over others.
- It is your responsibility to ensure the safety of all students. You should be watching and aware of all students' movements in the classroom, hallway, cafeteria, and playground, not only to prevent possible health hazards or accidents but to be aware of bullying as well. Any activity that appears threatening or dangerous should be reported to the school administration and/or school resource officer.
- You should be acquainted with all legal and ethical considerations for the teaching profession. Familiarize yourself with your legal responsibility to report possible abuse and neglect of a student and the proper channels to do so.
- You should have full control over your responses to students and other teachers. Emotional responses and outbursts of anger aimed either at a student or simply an irritating situation have no place

Insight 24

in the classroom. Since chaotic conditions occur frequently in the school setting, teachers need to practice coping mechanisms so that they do not display unprofessional behavior in front of the students. Professionalism also involves voice control. You should never scream or try to talk above your students.

Regardless of the grade level taught, it is important to remember that you are modeling professionalism for your students' to display in the future. One day your students may be in a profession and one of the only places that they learn professionalism is in the school environment. High standards in your work and behavior inspire students.

Remember: Students expect us to act in a professional manner and are motivated by our conduct.

In the classroom students not only learn the subject matter you present, but they absorb the ideals you display in your behavior in the classroom, at school activities, and in the community as well.

Remember: Values are caught, not taught.

Insight 25
Nonverbal Cues

There is a story of a college psychology professor who required a project from each student. As the professor lectured, he had a habit of pacing back and forth in front of the class. One of the students contacted all the class members with an idea for a full-class project in behavior modification.

For the next few weeks, as the professor lectured and paced across the front of the room, the students on the right side of the class paid attention, took notes, made eye contact, and otherwise made it obvious by their nonverbal cues that they were hanging onto every word the professor uttered. But, when he paced to the left of the class, the students' apathetic body language, lack of eye contact, and a general disinterest in what he was saying was apparent. Eventually, the professor stopped his pacing and remained on the right side of the class.

A large part of communication is nonverbal. Our ancestors communicated in this manner long before language was developed. After the evolution of languages, nonverbal communication became a way to share information with people who spoke different languages. Much of our modern communication is nonverbal as well, even if we are unaware of it: gestures such as nodding or shaking of the head, shrugging the shoulders, furrowing the brow or rolling the eyes, avoidance of eye contact, arms crossed in front of the body, or slouching in a chair, just to name a few examples.

Remember: The average person has over 7,000 facial expressions.

Insight 25

Everyone with close family ties learns to read nonverbal cues. We can tell if a spouse, parent, sibling, or child is in a good or bad mood after just a few seconds observing their body language or facial expressions.

Body language can be interpreted as aggressive or defensive, interested or disinterested. When we speak, our tone can be soothing or sarcastic. We can speak loudly or softly with well-placed pauses. Paralinguistic tone and loudness of voice can be misinterpreted, regardless of the words spoken. All of these communicate feelings and intentions.

Students are very astute in translating nonverbal cues from the teacher. A shrug of the shoulders, smirk of the lips, or shakes of the head can speak negative volumes to a student. The eyes can indicate complete attentiveness by prolonged eye contact or a cynical, sarcastic eye roll. Also, not looking at someone when you talk can communicate disinterest in that person. Be aware of your responses to a student, and make sure you convey respect for and interest in your students' comments and behavior.

It is also very important not to send conflicting cues. You may be saying one thing but your body language is communicating something totally different. In this situation, the student may interpret your motives as being dishonest. Since body language is generally thought of as being unconscious behavior, the student will believe your body's communication when you send mixed signals.

A student also communicates to you in the same manner. By reading nonverbal cues you can discern if a student understands the concept you are teaching or if they appear totally lost. You can also tell if a student is feeling bad, anxious, or disturbed in some way. By developing your ability to read nonverbal communication you can possibly address any feelings or situations the student is trying to communicate. His body language will teach you about his true feelings.

Remember: You are the only certified teacher in the room, but you are not the only teacher.

Humans have a built-in protective response to any new environment. When we walk into any situation, our brains immediately scan for danger. The logical portions of our brains (the cerebrum) makes its decisions based on what the emotional brain (the limbic system) relays. These emotional areas of our brains will communicate with our cognitive areas if there is some perceived threat. We are not necessarily aware of this process until our brains stimulate our fight-or-flight response and we begin to feel anxious and fearful.

When your students enter your classroom, they will automatically look at you to discern your mood. If they perceive a negative emotion because of your body language or facial expressions, their minds will be less receptive to the lessons for the day because their alarm system will be activated. You may not even be aware of the signals you are displaying. Maybe the previous class crawled all over your nerves, or you had a flat tire on the way to work. Regardless of the reason, you need to avoid carrying negative baggage into your classes. Be intentional about displaying postitive facial expressions and body language.

Remember: Teachers have to become good actors. It is very important for a teacher to train himself to convey positive nonverbal communication.

Teachers should practice conveying positive body language communications. Some tips are as follows:

- Make eye contact when you speak to your students.
- Be aware of your tone when speaking. What does your voice convey? Students respond to confidence. As their leader, you make your students more comfortable when they feel that you have a plan and know where you are leading them. Confidence relaxes them, and they feel safe enough to learn. But understand there is a difference between confidence and arrogance. Avoid communicating either verbally or nonverbally an inflated self-importance.
- Keep your shoulders back. Don't slump.
- Balance your weight on both feet.
- Avoid repeating the same gestures throughout your discussion. Some teachers tend to "talk with their hands," and they look like

they are leading a choral ensemble. Repeated mannerisms will quickly turn students off or distract them.

One area of positive body language is to teach your students nonverbal signals to communicate silent requests, such as the need for a bathroom or water break. A hand signal for "I don't understand" or "please repeat" will allow shy students to communicate directly with the teacher, and it cuts down on classroom disruption. We are all aware of a student's raising his hand in order to ask a question, a universal sign that students learn early in their school experience. You can teach other signals besides hand-raising that are specific to your classroom.

Remember: Nonverbal signals can help shy students communicate with the teacher.

Insight 26

Documentation

When you are dealing with students, parents, and administration, the three major rules are document, document, and document. Some schools and grade levels will require that you keep a folder for each student, especially if the student has an IEP—individualized education plan. Even if you have students who do not have an IEP or some other required documentation, keeping a folder is a wonderful tool for you to track student progress. Proper documentation is also needed when communicating with administrators, counselors, and parents. Unfortunately, there may be situations in which documentation is needed by law enforcement, hopefully not because of your actions, but to validate a student's behavior.

Remember: Always document *all* interactions with parents and especially all disciplinary events with students. A parent can argue with your memory of a child's behavior, but they cannot argue with a written discipline log.

Shortly after receiving your class roll, you need to make a physical folder for every student you will be teaching that year. Creating a virtual folder on your computer as a place to save emails from a student's parents and information from administration and counselors is an excellent idea you should utilize, and there will also be plenty of hard-copy paperwork concerning your students that will need to be filed, so you will need to have a physical file folder as well.

Any interaction with a student that you feel may involve future disciplinary referrals should be recorded. The more information an administrator has concerning a student's activities and behavior in your classroom, the more helpful it will be if the administrator has to confront the student and parents about a situation. Be sure to use specific terms when speaking of a student's behavior: Avoid vague references such as "Johnny was mean to other students." Explain the action. "Johnny struck another student on the arm with a ruler." Avoid the mention of another student's name in your report.

Your documentation will not always be for disciplinary purposes. It is a helpful resource to a counselor or school medical official if you record any behavioral changes you may notice in a student. Does she seem excessively anxious, and in what manner? Is he sleeping in class? Has there been an increase in bathroom visits? Do you have reason to believe that the student is being bullied? Explain your comments in detail.

One aspect of a teacher's documentation is the grade book. School districts require their teachers to keep an electronic grade book using a computer program supplied by the school district. This electronic record allows the administration access to how a student is progressing in your class at any given time. Keeping a hard-copy grade book as backup is highly advisable as well since electronic programs may fail. A printout of the online grade book can be placed in a three ring binder or individual student printouts can be placed in the student's folder. Some teachers prefer a hand-written record book. Either way, a backup is always an excellent plan.

Each school district will have a standard grading scale. It is important that you adhere to the prescribed scale and that your grading documentation reflects the district code. There may be a situation when you have to leave your job midyear and your grades and folders are turned over to a replacement teacher. An easy transition will occur if your records are clear and adhere to district standards.

As with any type of documentation, it's always important to consider your time and energy. As a teacher, you will be spending plenty of your time at school and at home time grading papers and creating lesson plans. Documenting classroom activities, grades, parent communications, and student behavior, as vital as it may be, is just another addition to your already stressed workload.

Therefore, you will need to schedule documentation time, a time when interruptions are at a minimum so that mistakes are not made. Records of grades and events are only as good as their accuracy. If your home life is a place of constant interruption, consider staying later after school to complete this task. This will also decrease the amount of work you have to take home.

How long should you keep student records after they have left your class? You should ask your administrator this question to see if there is a standard amount of time before you should keep records before destroying them. The most important records for a teacher to keep would be disciplinary documents and referrals as well as correspondence with parents concerning their child. Grades can be kept, but most schools have digital records of student grades, so whether to keep additional grade records would be up to the teacher.

The only legal standards a teacher must consider are student privacy laws. All records—current and past—need to be secured so that only the teacher, counselors, and administrators have access. Once the time limits established by your school are up, shred all sensitive documents.

Insight 27

Parent Conferences

ONE AREA WHERE NEW TEACHERS CAN GET SWEATY PALMS AND ANXIety attacks is the parent-teacher conference. As scary as it may be, conferences are a fact of life for a teacher, and if you are prepared, these interactions will go smoothly and can be beneficial to you, the parent(s), and the student. There are several types of meetings you will be involved in with parents. In all cases, be prepared with any information that the meeting may require. Also, make sure your attitude at the conference is positive: You and the parent(s) are meeting to decide the best course of action for the student.

Remember: Preparation prevents perspiration.

Here are various types of parent-teacher meetings that will occur throughout the school year:

- Meet the teacher: At the beginning of the school year, there will most likely be a day when the parents and students are allowed to come to the school and meet the teacher. These meetings are rather informal and simply allow the parents to "put a face to the name" of their child's teacher. Since no instruction has yet occured, there will be no discussion of grades or discipline problems. If school has started, and your school has a Meet the Teacher Night, limit your discussions. If the parents want to talk about grades or behavior, have them schedule a meeting with you through the guidance office.

Meet the Teacher gives you an opportunity to give parents and students information about your class, such as supplies that students need, grading expectations, projects that may be assigned, and any expectations you have of students.

A meet-and-greet environment provides an excellent opportunity to make a positive impression on parents and students. Even though this is an informal meeting you must dress in a professional manner. It is a good idea to speak with students about hobbies they may enjoy and just get to know them for a few minutes. Since this event is very informal, other parents will be in line to speak with you, so keep it brief and pleasant.

- Private face-to-face meeting with the parent(s): This meeting has been called because it will involve some sort of correction that needs to take place—poor grades or behavioral issues, or possibly both. In this environment, it is important to be prepared with documentation of the student's actions and grades.

The personal parent conference is usually called because of a request from either the parent(s) or the teacher. Be sure your request for a conference is made directly to the parent(s) (through an email or phone call) and not through a note sent home by the student. It may never arrive.

Keep in mind that the purpose of the meeting is to discuss if the student has met your expectations and to give suggestions on how improvement can occur. Always begin a conference of this nature with several positive comments about the student. This meeting is not a time to vent your frustrations without suggestions for improvement. The parent(s) may also voice their frustrations regarding their child and possibly the teacher as well. This is a good reason to include the guidance counselor in the meeting. "I need your help" is a powerful statement to make certain the parent(s) understands that she is involved in the student's education. If for some reason the conversation cannot be directed toward a positive outcome, you have the right to end the meeting and refer the parent(s) to your principal for further discussion.

Remember: Parents and teachers are on the same team.

- Parent email conferences: Some parents will prefer to correspond through email because their schedules conflict with your schedule and a face-to-face meeting is not convenient. In this case, make sure all communication is very clear, and print the emails as documentation. Be certain to stick to the facts and not opinions. A follow-up phone call would also be a good idea, just to verify that all communication was understood.
- Counselor-led conferences: In these conferences there is a school counselor present to facilitate the meeting. These consultations usually involve all of the student's teachers, but it is possible that it will just be with one teacher. All of the above suggestions apply in these meetings. Continue to document the outcome of the meeting, even though the counselor will also make notes.

Remember: Parents have an emotional investment in their children. Keep this in mind when communicating.

It is very helpful to use the "good-bad-good" approach. Begin by telling the parent(s) some positive observations you have about their child. At this point you can segue into the negative behavior or academic performance and end with a nice supportive statement. All parents wish to hear good things about their children; there will always be something positive to say about any child you teach. At the end of the conference, be sure to thank the parent(s) for their support.

INSIGHT 28

Teacher Burnout and Rewiring Your Brain

NEW TEACHERS DON'T THINK ABOUT BURNOUT, BUT IT IS SOMETHING that you need to guard against, even in the early years of your career. Often, burnout, an emotional condition, occurs well into a teacher's career, but factors that lead to burnout begin long before symptoms appear.

What exactly is burnout? It is a psychological condition of emotional exhaustion that manifests itself in low morale and decreased self-esteem as well as a decline in professional achievement.

In the brain, neural circuits change, making stressful situations harder to manage. Your emotional brain, or limbic system, interprets stress and danger, and it signals the prefrontal cortex of the cerebrum. In a low-stress environment, healthy neural communication occurs, but in chronic stressful situations, communication is not received properly. This reactive part of your brain increases its neural pathways and makes it easier to send signals to the cortex. Because of these increased connections, the perception of the stressfulness of the event can be greater than it is in reality.

Chronic stress changes the structure of the brain, leading to decreased cognitive skills, memory, and creativity. These stressors can include a feeling of being out of control. Having increased state and district mandates can leave you feeling out of control. These requirements and unreasonable timelines contribute to a greater workload, making you feel helpless and unable to be creative in your own classroom. There can be a feeling that

Insight 28

you are never going to be caught up with work. These negative feelings may give you an impression that you are not effective in the classroom.

There is a relationship between teacher burnout and student motivation. As mentioned in an earlier insight, your body language communicates things to your students. A perception of ineffectiveness manifests itself as depression. The students' perceptions of your well-being can add to behavioral issues and affect learning. To compound the problem, you may feel unproductive and think that student behavior problems and decreased motivation are your fault. The sense of decreased self-worth and being unvalued, as well as an added workload from administration, can possibly cause you to isolate yourself from colleagues. It is at this time that a support group of fellow professionals becomes vital in keeping you grounded.

There are several habits that effective teachers use to help combat burnout:

- Train your brain to leave survival mode. Get away from the stressful environment for a period of time. Leaving is not always possible if you are in the middle of a school year or semester, but planning some mini-vacation time can help.
- If getting away is not an option, scheduling a balance of rest and exercise can help. If you don't schedule this time, other activities will get in the way and your relaxation will not happen. The main idea is to free your mind from the issues of work. Take up a relaxing hobby, enjoy your favorite music, or go for a walk in nature. Make it a priority to carve out some time for yourself to relax and debrief. Read a novel or a book that is not related to teaching.
- Spend some time with friends and make it a rule not to talk about your jobs. Keep conversations positive.
- Within the school environment, all teachers need to feel appreciated and respected. Get involved in helping develop ways that you and your colleagues can work together to lower some of the demands you face. Make it clear to the administration that all teachers simply need time to complete tasks.

You will find that by implementing some of the above ideas, your confidence in the classroom will return and your students will respond in a positive way. From that point on, make it a priority to take care of yourself.

Remember: Find ways to express your creative skills and feel valued for the job you do, and burnout may be avoided.

Insight 29

Morning Person

Are you an early bird or a night owl? There are those teachers who get to school early and have papers sorted and pencils sharpened well before the school bell rings. Of course, there are also those who sit in their cars drinking their last sips of coffee before climbing out of the front seat and slowly walking across the parking lot, staring at the pavement. And then there's everyone else, who fall somewhere in between these extremes. Scientists call this behavior your "chronotype," derived from the word *chronology*, which deals with an individual's time-of-day preference.

When studying chronotypes, scientists found that "early birds" tend to go to sleep earlier and get up earlier, while "night owls" do just the opposite. Interestingly, the desire for morning or evening has nothing to do with sleep duration. Both chronotypes may get the same number of sleep hours but the early risers are more bright-eyed in the morning than the other group. Some biological studies have shown a difference in brain serotonin levels during the morning hours as compared to the afternoon, and many researchers believe that the difference is encoded into DNA, making the behavior very difficult to alter. It's also important to point out that most people fall somewhere on a sleep-wake spectrum. Not everyone is an early bird or a night owl. Too, it appears that chronotypes can change with age.

School systems and society in general tend to favor morning people. Unfortunately, this preference makes night people appear lazy, and it can affect their mental and physical health. The major question is this:

Insight 29

Can a night person train to become a morning person? Even though a person can't alter their genetics, there are environmental factors that they can change. The following hints can help teachers who tend not to be morning people or parents of students who have trouble getting going in the morning:

- Work at slowly shifting your sleep-wake times, creating an earlier-to-bed earlier-to-rise situation. Don't expect your body to respond right away. This change takes time. Alter your bedtime and wake time by small increments, like 15 to 20 minutes at a time every few days. It is important to keep a consistent schedule.
- Develop a nightly routine. Limit exposure to bright lights one hour before bed. Light blocks melatonin (the hormone that induces sleep) production in the brain.
- Get more light in the morning. Light inhibits melatonin production and helps us wake up.
- At night, develop calming patterns such as deep breathing or reading a book (not an eBook but a hard-copy one). Turn off back-lit screens such as those on cell phones and tablets.
- Don't eat late at night, and refrain from sugary foods and caffeine 4 to 6 hours before your established bedtime.
- Drink a glass of water soon after leaving your bed. We breathe all night, and for each breath, we lose water. Often our sluggish feelings are actually dehydration.
- Never skip breakfast. After you wake in the morning your pancreas produces extra insulin, which lowers blood sugar. If you don't replace the nutrients, you may feel sluggish. Breakfast should include protein and whole grains, *not* processed sugar. Proper foods will keep your blood sugar level throughout the morning and sustain your energy through midmorning.
- Drink a lot of water between classes because water boosts energy. Dehydration leads to fatigue: It impacts the flow of oxygen to the brain and causes your heart to work harder to pump oxygenated

blood to all your organs, making you more tired and less alert. By staying hydrated throughout the day, you stay energized.

Neither teachers nor students have control over the school schedule. If you tend to be a night owl, it will be in your best interest to practice these suggestions and attempt to alter your chronotype as much as possible. Your daily activities, such as exercise, diet, and socialization, can help you reinforce any changes you have made to your chronotype. But give it time. Change of this sort does not happen quickly.

Remember: When changing your sleep patterns, consistency is key.

When you identify students who appear inactive and sleepy in your morning classes, consider sharing the above strategies with their parents in the hope that they can become more alert and not miss out on instruction. If your school allows students to bring their personal water bottles, have students take very short water breaks. This strategy can be used at a time when students have become restless, unfocused, or a little noisy. A water break can be a calming tool.

INSIGHT 30

Relationships with Fellow Teachers

A NEW TEACHER'S FIRST JOB WILL PROBABLY BEGIN WITH AN ADMINIStrator's personal tour of the school, involving the physical layout of the school and introductions to many of the people who will eventually offer help and support. Hopefully you will be introduced to a "buddy teacher." As a fledgling teacher, connecting with a strong, experienced teacher can make all the difference in making your first years a success. Many administrators know the value of this relationship and will pair you with a colleague who may teach the same grade level and subject. But if that doesn't happen, ask your administrator for the names of strong teachers whom you can have a mentoring relationship with or seek a mentor—particularly one that has taught for five years or more—to learn from and lean on.

Mentors can offer valuable feedback and help you see situations from a different perspective, preventing you from taking failures personally or making too much out of a situation. A mentor can help you celebrate your successes and give you someone to vent to in tough times. They can help you grow.

A new teacher needs to achieve a comfort level with a potential mentor before asking for help and assistance. Since a teacher is often the only professional in the classroom and possibly the only adult—unless a teacher aide is assigned to assist—some teachers tend to see their jobs as a solitary and autonomous profession. Because of this self-sufficient attitude toward their job, teachers may be resistant to reaching out for help. But don't make the mistake of not choosing a mentor.

It may be more comfortable to first cultivate your relationship with a colleague so that you see her as your professional equal. Get to know this teacher on a personal level. Often, what begins as a professional relationship will blossom into a friendship that you will cherish throughout your career, even if you part ways and move to other schools. Some of the longest-lasting friendships you will ever have in your life will come from your time as a teacher.

Never discount the value of learning from teachers of other disciplines. Cross-curriculum discussions and teamwork can offer unique insights into many of the problems you face. You may also be surprised to find out that a difficult student in your class might be a joy in another. Learn from other teachers.

Remember: Teaching is a collaborative profession. Soak up all the wisdom you can from more experienced teachers.

During the school day, every teacher, regardless of their years of experience, needs a refuge away from students. We established in the introduction that you will develop a love for your students; however, you will also crave and need adult conversation during your teaching day. The teachers' lounge can be the best or worst place to be: a respite from the trials of the day or a wasp's nest of gossip and complaints.

Find a positive environment where you can discuss concerns and interests with like-minded teachers rather than absorb the negativity from complaints and the stress from toxic conversation. Of course, how and when you interact with other teachers will depend on your schedule and your school's environment. Just make sure you're in an encouraging atmosphere.

Remember: Toxic conversations will deplete your creative energies. Seek out positive environments and relationships.

One area that is open to all teachers are online teacher forums. Through this medium, you can share experiences and get advice from educators who teach the same subject and grade level literally all over the globe. View online teacher forums as an addition to your interpersonal relationships you have developed within your school. It would be a mistake to detach from others within your school and commit yourself totally to the online world.

Be proud you are a teacher. Never forget why you chose this profession. It obviously wasn't for the money or even the free time. It was to make a difference in the lives of young people. You have chosen a noble profession. Your influence will carry on after you in ways that you can only imagine.

Remember: Be proud of your contribution to the future.

Appendix A
Insightful Teacher Experiences

THE FOLLOWING STORIES ARE TRUE EXPERIENCES SHARED BY TEACHERS. These humorous stories will hopefully provide insights and bits of wisdom to help teachers navigate the everyday events of their classrooms.

Losing His Marbles

If opportunity knocks, at least peek out the door. Teachers are opportunists. They will take any opportunity to create a proper teaching environment when the chance arises. In other words, they do whatever they can to keep the students quiet. The beginning of a school year is particularly a challenge since it's a well-known fact that students will test their teachers. The students need to know just how strict their teacher is and if they really mean what they say.

One ninth-grade science teacher's third period class was a spirited bunch, to say the least. On this day, early in the school year, the particular lab he had planned was tedious, requiring the students' full attention. After two, three, or maybe a dozen attempts to calm the class by the futile method of asking them to be quiet, he reached for any object on his lab counter that was large enough to be used as a makeshift gavel. Sometimes an out-of-place noise will get the attention of the class, at least long enough for them to see whether or not something is blowing up.

He picked up a jar half full of marbles. The plan was to tap the jar on the table, much like someone gently striking a spoon to a goblet at a dinner party before a toast. Who knows, maybe he had some subliminal desire to smash the jar against the wall, or maybe it was simply physics; but as the glass came down on the lab counter, the marbles flew up, and the jar exploded. Marbles sailed in every direction, bouncing endlessly on the hard tile of the laboratory floor. The bottom of the broken jar shattered on the table while he held the rest of the jagged slivers in his hand. The pinging of the marbles seemed to go on forever.

Then there was silence. A deafening quiet, the likes of which has never been experienced in a public school classroom. No one moved. His students' eyes were as big as dinner plates. At that very moment, he stood at the crossroads. He could confess that he didn't really mean to break the jar, or he could use this situation to his advantage. Opportunity knocked!

The teacher stood in front of the class and matched their silence. Then, when he began to speak, his voice was slow and clear.

Part of the way through his impromptu sermon, he noticed some of the students staring in horror at the floor beside his feet. Red spatters were creating a puddle on the lab floor from blood dripping from his palm. Again, opportunity knocked! He closed his hand and slowly strolled past the wide-eyed students to the first-aid kit on the back wall of the lab. During his casual walk, he continued talking, expounding on how the students should develop proper listening skills and how this would be a valuable asset to their future.

While he wrapped his hand in gauze, he noticed four students had taken it upon themselves to crawl on the floor to pick up marbles; however, they never took a watchful eye off the teacher. They never spoke. To be honest, that class never spoke another word all year.

The teacher learned two lessons that day: When opportunity knocks, turn any situation into a teachable moment. And don't mess with breakable objects when you're in a high state of anxiety.

His students learned a valuable lesson that day as well: Watch out for the crazy science teacher!

Passing Papers

In the classroom, there are procedures that anyone who can read this sentence has done. Every student has sat in a classroom and passed papers back. The teacher gives a small stack to the person in the front row, and they, in turn, take one and pass the rest back. It's usually a routine course of action where little explanation is needed. At least, that's what this teacher used to think, until one day in her middle school math class.

One morning she handed "Johnny" a stack of papers, and then continued to the next row until all the worksheets were distributed.

She thought.

The classroom quieted, and she took advantage of the time to complete her attendance sheets.

After about ten minutes, a student on Johnny's row asked, "What are we supposed to be doing?"

"You mean after you finish the worksheet?" the teacher responded.

"What worksheet?"

"The sheets I gave Johnny to pass—" and then she noticed that no one on the row had any sheets and Johnny was just working his little heart out.

"Johnny?"

"Yes, Ma'am?"

"Um . . . did you not pass back any sheets for the others on your row?"

"I thought they were all mine," he said, looking rather bewildered at the three sheets he had already completed.

She promptly gave the students behind him their sheets and told them that they could do them for homework, since we were ready to move to the next assignment. She told Johnny to turn in one of the three sheets. Problem solved.

She thought.

Just like an episode from some lawyer show, all the students on Johnny's row approached the teacher's desk.

"That's not fair! Everyone else got to do it in class, now we have homework!"

"But didn't you wonder what everyone else was doing?" she asked.

One of the girls shrugged.

"I should get credit for all three papers, since I did extra work," said Johnny.

"Didn't you notice some similarity in those papers?" she asked.

He shrugged.

"Johnny, you turn in one paper, and the rest of you have yours done tomorrow."

"That's not fair!" the girl whined.

The teacher shrugged.

NEVER TURN YOUR BACK

In the teaching world, there are few jobs tougher than practice teaching. It was during that tough time, on one particular day, that a practice teacher learned to face the students. Always. This was the day his pants split.

The teacher was practicing in an honors biology class when, for some reason, his backside began to feel rather odd. Maybe it was the sixth sense that teachers develop, or the cold winter day beginning to seep in; but he felt the need to inspect the seat of his pants. While the students worked, he discreetly brushed his hand across the back of his pants. The material felt dangerously thin, to say the least.

For the remainder of that class period, the teacher did most of his instructing from a stool, asking students to come to the board and write sentences and draw diagrams. This approach seemed like a wonderful teaching method, one that involved active participation from the students. As they walked past him to the blackboard, he scanned their faces for any evidence that they were aware of his predicament. He saw none.

Now, after many years of teaching experience, this teacher has learned that teenagers don't possess the ability to keep information of this magnitude to themselves. If one is too shy to approach the subject, they will surely tell another, who will tell another, until the class clown falls into the chain of gossip. At which time, it will become public knowledge. Since there were no outbursts, no comments, no jokes, his secret was safe.

Finally, after what seemed like an entire career in teaching, the period ended and he bolted for the men's room. As suspected, the entire backside of his pants was not only split, but frayed as well. He had two more classes to go and his home was too far from the school to make changing clothes an option. It was time to improvise.

With the proper school supplies, a person can face almost any emergency. He could even perform minor surgery, if the situation arose. Since he had on brown pants, only one option seemed feasible: He folded some brown paper towels and stapled them along the inside of his pants. Problem solved.

To help conceal this secret, he wore his sport jacket the rest of the day—because of the cold weather, of course. He may have been the teacher who coined the phrase, "Never turn your back on the students." Now you know why.

Let's Go Outside!

"Today, we're having class outside." For the students, it doesn't get any better than that. Unless the teacher says, "Y'all go on home," the students could never be more excited. The great outdoors is a perfect resource to aid any curriculum; however, it usually evokes visions of teenagers running wildly across campus, battling with acorns and, in general, not listening to a thing the teacher says.

Science teachers have a multitude of opportunities to use the outdoors in their classes. After all, when we study nature, where's the best place to be? In nature! On one such occasion, nature followed this teacher back into the classroom and taught everyone a lesson.

"What is this, Miss. B?" The girl rushed out of the goldenrod field carrying a tan cocoon-like object. It looked as if it were made of papier-mâché.

"Ah, now, that is a nice find!" Miss B said.

The student smiled brightly while the rest of the class gathered around, elbowing for a position.

"This is the egg case of a praying mantis." Miss B explained how the female mantis lays a case full of eggs in the fall because she won't survive the winter, but her young will hatch in the spring.

Then came the questions. "Can we take it back and hatch 'em?"

"How long does it take?"

Miss B was soon to learn a lesson about tampering with nature.

Appendix A

She agreed to take the egg case to the classroom and continued her lesson by explaining how gardeners like to collect the cases and place them among their plants because the praying mantis is a beneficial insect.

Mission accomplished. The students were excited about their outdoor find and eager to learn more about this insect. They put the case in a prominent place in the classroom and waited for spring and the birth of a new generation.

Autumn gave way to winter and the case was shoved aside, virtually forgotten, while the class studied other subjects and readied themselves for semester exams. Christmas came and went, and the students settled into the doldrums of January, where the possible promise of a snow day is about all that will excite a student.

Then their lesson began. As a science teacher, Miss B still blushes at her ignorance of the obvious. Yes, she was correct in saying that the egg case would hatch in the spring. She was thinking of the time needed for the maturation of the young as well as the lengthening of the day. But what stimulates the hatching? Heat.

Her classroom tended to be hot. Even on twenty-degree days, she would open her window. It was the end of the last week in January and all the proper conditions were met.

Over the weekend, the eggs hatched.

Earlier in the fall, Miss B had explained to her students the difference between complete and incomplete metamorphosis. These eggs would not produce larvae. The baby insects would look like the adults, only smaller. And they did. Thousands of them.

Monday morning brought an eerie surprise. Every tabletop and every desk had miniature praying mantises creeping along like tiny mechanical monsters from a Spielberg film. She was sweeping them into a dustpan when the first students arrived. Two girls immediately screamed and ran from the room. One sleepy boy plopped down in his desk, totally oblivious to the infestation on his backside. When he stood, the rear of his jeans looked like a piece of abstract art using stick men as its subject.

Several brave students helped brush armies of marching mantises into jars and boxes, while most of the class cowered at the door, asking if we were going to call off school. They eventually dumped the creatures out the window and attempted to resume class.

For the rest of the school year, someone would occasionally find a tiny mantis carcass stuck to some tape or dangling from an old cobweb on the ceiling tile.

The following autumn, Miss B had a new class and they went outside for a nature study.

"Hey, look what I found!" exclaimed a boy when he walked out of the goldenrod field.

Miss B pointed to the goldenrod field, "Go put that back! We don't mess with Mother Nature!"

What's in a Name? A Lot!

A new teacher doesn't take long to learn the importance of calling students by name. Especially the correct name! One teacher had to apologize profusely after calling Geoff, "Gee-off," on the first day of school. That was an embarrassing mistake; yet often it's not the teacher's fault. Another first-of-the-year roll call dialogue went something like this:

"Johnny Jones."

"Present," responded the student.

"Sally Smith."

"Present."

"Charlie Rogers."

"Randolph," came a voice from the back of the room.

The teacher paused and looked up. "I'm sorry. Is the name Randolph?"

"No. Charlie done 'rand-off.' Nobody knows where he is."

And on goes the battle to get the roll correct without scarring a student for life.

Learning names is much easier once the teacher can connect a personality with a student. However, this leads to a little-known phenomenon called *new teacher pregnancy*. Now, don't misunderstand. This phenomenon only means that teachers new to the profession seem to start their families very early. To the untrained, the reason for this may appear to be that teachers have an extended summer vacation, which is a

Appendix A

perfect time for beginning a family. The truth is this: If you wait too many years to have your own children, all the names are used up. Every name you consider for your kids reminds you of a student!

Things Our Contract Does NOT Say

A teacher's contract for the school system is very clear. Few teachers doubt what they are supposed to do as classroom teachers. Each spring, teachers sign a contract for the next school year. Teachers rarely question what the school district expects of them; however, occasionally it's a good idea to pull the paperwork from the file drawer and check the fine print, just to make sure. One teacher, Mr. Johnson, leaves it lying on his podium next to his reading glasses. Just in case.

Mr. Johnson began to take attendance when a student walked to his podium.

"Mr. J? Do you think I have a fever?" the student asked.

"Well, I really can't tell. Why? Do you feel sick?"

"I feel hot. Does my face feel hot to you?"

"Uh, well, let me see." Mr. Johnson reluctantly placed the back of his hand on the student's forehead. "It's hard to say. Why do you think you have a fever?"

His face contorted. "Well, I've been throwing up all morning."

Thank goodness for antibacterial soap! Mr. Johnson immediately rushed to the lab and washed all the way to his elbows twice, as if preparing for surgery. Getting a stomach virus is *not* in the contract. But he checked anyway.

On that particular day, the biology class was dissecting a frog. For obvious reasons Mr. J excused the sick boy from the day's activity and sent him to the school nurse. Making those decisions was a part of his employment agreement. He checked. But during that same period, that very same legal document was put to the test.

The dissections were well under way.

"Mr. J, I need some help over here." A young man on the other side of the lab gestured to the teacher. Mr. J hurried to his side, ready to point out the frog's pancreas or lift the liver and display the gall bladder. But then the student stepped back from the table, holding his gloved hands in the air.

Now, understand that this student's desire in life must have been to be a rap artist, or, at the very least, to dress like one. The crotch of his pants hung below his knees, and his belt was undone, much like everyone's Grandpa after a Thanksgiving dinner.

"Mr. J. My pants are falling down. Can you pull 'em up for me?"

Mr. Johnson hurried to his podium and slid on his reading glasses.

"Nope. I don't have to do that. I checked."

WHOA, NELLIE! ANOTHER FIELD TRIP!

Kindergarten is a time to experience the world. It's a time for a child to run free and leave life's worries and anxieties to the wringing hands of parents and teachers. The unbridled enthusiasm of a five-year-old can't be matched, unless, of course, you consider the truly unbridled race of a hay wagon across a plantation lawn. Here's the story.

Before Mr. Ballard felt the nudge to become a teacher, he was living in Charleston, South Carolina, while his wife was finishing school. He was employed at Middleton Plantation as a stable hand. Mr. Ballard spent the days caring for the horses, mules, and other farm animals, and he would occasionally hook up the fringed surrey and give visitors a tour of the twelve-acre lawn behind the main house. It was such a wonderful job that he didn't mind the low pay and high humidity. Even having to dress in authentic colonial wear was worth the opportunity for him to work closely with the farm animals.

But one aspect of the job he learned to fear: kindergarten school field trips.

One beautiful spring morning, after he had hitched two mules to the hay wagon, he helped a kindergarten teacher and three mothers load fifteen five-year-olds onto the back of the hay wagon. Then the ladies decided to let young Mr. Ballard be the sole chaperone on this part of the field trip. They waved vigorously to the youngsters as the wagon took off, creaking and groaning across the ruts in the dirt road. As the sleepy mules pulled the wagon under draperies of Spanish moss, the children stared over the sideboard at a herd of sheep grazing on the plantation lawn. This trip was going to be easy. Mr. Ballard settled back and breathed in the thick, Low Country morning air.

After a while, these kids had been so well behaved that Mr. Ballard decided to lengthen the trip a little before heading back to the stables. He pulled the wagon near the wall that separated the plantation lawn from Highway 61. But just then a pickup truck backfired.

Now, most people know that mules don't like sudden loud noises. Immediately, all four ears laid back and the mules took off as if they were contenders for the Kentucky Derby. Ballard stood and pulled on the reins with all his strength. He screamed all the while, "Whoa, Nellies, yees, and haws," and any other mule language that came to mind, but still they raced toward the stables. The four women watching the wagon hurtle toward them wore looks of pure terror on their faces.

It wouldn't have been so bad if the mules hadn't decided to take a shortcut under the two-hundred-year-old live oak trees. The problem wasn't the trees, but the roots. When the wagon wheels struck those enormous roots, the wagon began to bounce every which way a hay wagon full of kindergarten kids could bounce. At one point, Ballard glanced over his right shoulder and saw several airborne children crash headfirst into a bale of hay.

As expected, the mules calmed themselves once they reached the stable gate, and the four red-faced women flew to the side of the wagon. Just then one little boy screamed, "Let's do it again!"

As time passed, Mr. Ballard turned in his muddy boots and hay rake for comfortable shoes and chalk. But remember that certain subliminal fears remain embedded in the human brain. To this day, when a student says, "Let's go on a field trip!" Mr. Ballard immediately responds, "Whoa, Nellie!"

Who Threw the Pickle?

All teachers remember their very first day as classroom teachers. Ms. Bailey did not have a typical beginning because her career began at the end of the school year, not in August or September when most teachers start.

Appendix A

Two weeks before school was to be out, a teacher had left to take a job in industry, so she was hired to take his place in a seventh-grade science classroom. But it wasn't the classroom experience that she remembers so vividly from that first day. It was those two words that all teachers eventually come to hate: cafeteria duty!

After her third period class, her assignment was to supervise the first lunch period. No one told her that she had to do this alone. But actually, she wasn't alone. Ms. Bailey had about three hundred screaming middle school students to keep her company.

The first lesson that she learned was that kindergarten teachers waste a lot of time teaching their students to walk slowly in single file from place to place. By the time those students reach middle school, they have lost all the walking-in-single-file skills that they may have once possessed.

When the bell rang, a large hoard of preteens came barreling into the cafeteria as if someone had yelled, "Free ice cream!" Ms. Bailey quickly longed for her college days in animal husbandry when unruly heifers could be zapped with an electric prod. However, she assumed the administration would frown on that technique, so she resorted to the only means at her disposal. She screamed, "Slow down!" and "Get in line!" To put it mildly, that did not work.

Ms. Bailey couldn't line up a few hundred middle schoolers. She felt defeated, but she was about to feel much worse.

The cafeteria served raisins. As a science teacher, she saw a nutritious snack made from the dried fruit of a grape. The students saw something entirely different: artillery.

During her agricultural studies, she had often worked with honeybees. The site she witnessed that first day of her teaching career resembled a massive swarm of black killer bees hovering in the cafeteria. The airborne fruit created a dark cloud that appeared to be suspended in the air. Ms. Bailey can honestly attest to the fact that not one raisin was eaten during that lunch period.

Eventually, the bell rang and the students clamored out and down the hall to their next class, leaving the cafeteria empty and silent. Ms. Bailey stood in the corner in shock. The floor was covered with hundreds of tiny black dots. Just then, the principal walked in and surveyed the damage. He put his hands on his hips, shook his head, and left. No words were spoken. Ms. Bailey wiped away a tear, collected her clipboard and pen, and walked to the principal's office, totally aware that she had just experienced the shortest teaching career on record.

In the moments that followed, she wasn't fired. Actually, she received an apology. This was the very first day that raisins had ever been placed on the menu. Also, she was supposed to have help in the cafeteria but the helping teacher wasn't present that day.

Ms. Bailey admits that she felt a little better after her discussion with the principal. After all, there were some circumstances beyond her control. She will always recall the immortal words of a fellow teacher after a tough day of lunch duty when hamburgers were served. The fellow teacher walked up to her, and with the voice of frustration, created the battle cry for all teachers who are assigned cafeteria duty, "*I have a master's degree and I have to worry about who threw the pickle?*"

SCREAM FOR ICE CREAM

As the end of the year approaches, science teachers often prepare special "fun labs" for their students. But the teachers never tell the students that these activities actually combine core concepts learned all year long. It's best to let them think they are simply having a fun day, and then bring some learning in through the back door.

Students believe that the best science activities are labs that include eating. One particular chemistry teacher always ends the year with an ice cream lab. The students are challenged to form groups and determine which flavor and recipe is best for homemade churned ice cream.

Part of the assignment is for them to furnish everything they need. All the teacher provides is the ice. This assignment turns out to be a valuable lesson in group dynamics.

On more than one occasion, students brought all the ingredients, and the one group member assigned to bring the churn would walk in empty-handed and announce, "Was today when we were gonna make the ice cream?" It was all the teacher could do to keep the other group members from dousing him with milk, vanilla extract, and chocolate sprinkles.

On ice cream day, four or five churns would grind lazily while students scurried to pack ice around their prize-winning mixtures. Other class members lined cups and spoons across the lab counter and opened cans of chocolate syrup and packs of Oreo cookies. Everyone shared. Even teachers from other parts of the school stopped by the chemistry lab to be included in the taste test and helped vote for the best recipe. Some wonderful products came from the chemistry ice cream lab, but one concoction sent everyone who sampled it racing to the water fountain.

Details were not the strong point for one particular group of boys. They often worked together in lab, and *instructions* were merely *suggestions* to this crew; however, since this lab had to be consumed, the teacher hoped that they would give some serious thought to their recipe.
The group members showed up with the makings of a basic vanilla ice cream recipe and not some exotic brew. The boys produced measuring cups and directions handwritten by one of their grandmothers.

What could go wrong?

The electric churns toiled under the strain of packed ice, changing their tones as the cream got thicker. Soon, all the masterpieces were ready.

Each group huddled around their churns waiting for their first taste. The group of boys peeled off the churn top and scooped a spoonful into a paper cup.

"Mr. B, give ours a try," said one of the boys, addressing the chemistry teacher. No one else had taken a sample.

Mr. B cautiously placed the spoon into his mouth. His eyes widened and began to water. He tried with all his might not to contort his face, but the unmistakable taste burned his tongue.

Before Mr. B could say a word, one of the group members licked his spoon and screamed, "*That* is totally *gross*!"

At that proclamation, everyone came running. It seemed they all wanted to witness the teacher being poisoned.

"Um . . . guys? Did you put salt in this ice cream?" Asked Mr. B.

"Yeah, my grandma said she uses a whole box of this stuff when she makes ice cream." He held up a red, one-pound box of rock salt.

"Remember our discussion last class about the freezing point of water and how the salt is used with the *ice* to make the cream colder?" Reminded Mr. B.

Before he could answer, someone asked, "I thought y'all were making vanilla? This looks like chocolate!"

"Oh, yeah," one of the group members admitted, "the churn was kinda rusty. But we rinsed it out."

At that, they had the winner for the worst ice cream ever. They even named it Rusty Road. If the DMV were to spread this mixture over winter highways, there would never be slick roads on snow days!

SNOW DAY!

Take the excitement from all of the Christmas parties, Fall Festivals, and Spring Flings and measure it on a scale and it would never equal the sheer exhilaration that a kid gets from having a snow day. Ask your children on most evenings to watch the news and they will scurry to their rooms. But let the clouds thicken and the temperature drop on a January night and they will be glued to the TV, or their tablets and phones, praying to see those magic words pop up on the screen: Schools Are Closed! Even a two-hour delay will have them thanking the weatherman for their gift of a midweek Saturday morning.

At school, you can feel the excitement. The students think that a science teacher has some inside information into the weather. Before the late bell has sounded, every chemistry, physics, and biology teacher gets the same question: "Do you think it's going to snow?"

When the question is asked, the entire class falls silent as if waiting for a blessing from the Pontiff himself. If the teacher wants to grasp the teachable moment, he will expound at length about low-pressure systems and jet streams, or if feeling exceptionally devious, he can pass on the most accurate meteorological information there is: "I saw some snowbirds in my front yard!"

Once the flakes begin to fall, education is frozen as well. Most people think that the only reason we dismiss school is because of the dangers of icy roadways. Do we actually think that teenagers are going scurry home and watch the snow through frosted windowpanes while sipping hot chocolate with marshmallows? Of course not! They are going to be crammed into in any vehicle that can move and will be slipping and sliding all over the same treacherous roads that got them out of school. The fact is, we don't want them to get hurt, especially on school property.

The reality is, teachers are also excited by snow days. However, they are supposed to say things like, "We are just going to have to make it up," or "Do y'all want to go to school *all* summer?"

The lure of the snow day was once an unplanned gift from Mother Nature. However, today, the concept of the free snow day is not what it used to be. With e-learning days, many school districts require teachers to continue teaching through technology when school is out. So, sadly, the days of watching for snowbirds in your yard and grabbing your bread and milk from the store may be coming to an end.

These Kids Today

"I'm going to get real religious when I'm about sixty," claimed one student.

Teachers are never surprised at the statements they overhear from their students. All teachers tend to become inanimate fixtures in the halls, so students think as little about speaking in front of them as they might a brick wall.

At the lockers one teacher overheard a girl talking to her friend. "Do you have any perfume? I smell like deodorant."

At first, the teacher chuckled. Then she shook her head and said, "These kids today! Why, when I was their age—" and then she stopped. The students are simply reflecting what teachers and parents give them. The values of our society seep into these young people. Students tend to think that whenever they need to be responsible, moral, or dedicated, all they have to do is reach into their backpacks and pull out a fresh supply. There will always be some way to cover up a problem, or someone will come to the rescue. Where do these kids today get such crazy ideas?

One teacher shard this dialogue she had with a student's parent:

"Hello? Mrs. Smith? Your son is in my English class. I received a message that you wanted to talk to me."

"Yes, thank you for returning my call. I see that you gave my son a D in your class last quarter."

"Well, he came out with a 71 average."

"I don't understand this. He has always made straight As in English. Why wasn't I notified?"

"Mrs. Smith, the school sent out a progress report, and I sent home another report with your son just two weeks ago. Also, I had a talk with him concerning some work he never completed."

"I never saw either report. He never tells me anything. If you want me to know something, please don't send it with him because I'll never see it. He goes straight to work after school, you know."

"Is it possible for him to cut back on his job a little so he could have more time to study?" The teacher asked.

"Oh, don't I wish, but he has that car and insurance, you know. How can he make up the work or maybe do some extra credit, you know, to pull his grade up? I don't want this grade to affect his scholarship chances."

And so the cycle continues. It won't be long before a teacher overhears a student say, "When it's time for the SAT, I'm gonna get really smart!"

Appendix B

Always remember

Introduction: The Heart of a Teacher

- Teachers should always be lifelong learners.
- No seed ever sees the flower.

Insight 1: Monitor and Adjust

- Always have a Plan B.
- There are going to be interruptions beyond your control, so close your eyes, take three deep breaths, and accept it. Then be prepared.

Insight 2: Classroom Management—Rules and Corrections

- Teachers cause most behavior problems.
- Negative attention is still attention, so beware of the amount of responses you give to students who aren't showing expected behavior. You never want to reinforce poor behavior.
- It takes a school village to educate a child.
- Student behavior should never interfere with your teaching or a student's learning. Construct your classroom rules around this concept.
- Demonstrate positive behavior if you want your students to live up to your expectations.

- The number one classroom rule should be: "Please help me teach and others to learn."
- Until you're a seasoned teacher, many of your students have had more years giving teachers hard times than you have had teaching.
- You must be firm, yet flexible.
- To control, you don't have to be controlling.
- When rules are broken, it's not personal, so don't respond as if you've received a personal attack.

Insight 3: Teaching to Various Learning Styles

- Understanding that most teachers tend to teach in the manner that they were taught, a teacher must be intentional about having auditory, visual, *and* kinesthetic learning strategies.
- If a student is not learning from the way you teach, find out how they learn and change the way you teach. This might involve giving that student a learning styles inventory.
- Your delivery of information needs to be engaging and possibly entertaining, as well as brief.
- When designing a lesson, be sure to involve the three major learning styles in your instructional plan.

Insight 4: Everyone Learns at a different Rate

- The only dumb questions are the ones that were never asked.
- Always speak clearly and at the proper speed for students to understand.
- Always take a student from where they are to where you want them to be. Better yet, allow them to discover the path between old and new information.
- When students don't understand a concept it might not be their fault.

- Teachers need to acknowledge their students' effort, no matter how small.
- Human beings are built to learn.

Insight 5: Make the Material Relevant

- Learning is a building process.
- Students will respond best if they can relate to the material.

Insight 6: Consider the Needs of the Student

- Students learn best when they are physically comfortable.
- Teachers are expected to keep their students safe in the school building as well as on the playground and in common areas.
- Students need to feel valued and respected in order to learn.
- Create an environment of inclusion, not exclusion.
- You can help a student's self-esteem, but it takes time. Be patient.
- Success builds self-esteem.

Insight 7: The Teachable Moment—Time to Be Flexible

- The "learnable moment" may arise at any time. Allow yourself to be flexible.
- Always record your successes for future use and share them with other teachers.

Insight 8: Be a Servant Leader

- At one time you were sitting where they are now, so think about how you are perceived by your students.
- Be aware and listen to the nonverbal cues that students send you.

- When teachers listen to students' ideas, students can truly blossom.

Insight 9: There Is Something Very Important about a Name

- Names may have some familial or historical significance. Take your students' names seriously.
- Using a student's name communicates respect.
- Learn your students' names quickly and use them often.

Insight 10: Timing Is Important

- Never stop a lesson in the middle of a concept.
- Use time at the end of class to review that day's lesson.
- Develop strategies to use class time wisely.

Insight 11: Help Build a Better Brain through Repetition and Spacing

- Allowing proper time between concepts taught will enhance memory and retrieval of information.
- When students have ownership of their education, it will become more meaningful to them.
- Multitasking does not aid in learning.
- You need repetition when you want to strengthen memory and foster learning.

Insight 12: Forgetting Has Its Place in Learning

- Short-term forgetting can enhance long-term memory and recall.

Insight 13: Curiosity and Gap Instruction

- Don't simply tell, but allow for discovery.

- Prepare the students' minds first by allowing them to discover, make mistakes, retry, and succeed.

Insight 14: Teaching Machines versus Humans

- Multitasking decreases student comprehension, especially if the tasks are performed on a tablet or laptop.
- Handwritten note-taking is superior to laptop notation.
- The best educational strategy is always human to human.

Insight 15: Journaling Has Its Place in Any Subject

- Journaling inspires creativity, which leads to learning.
- Journaling needs to be a handwritten activity.
- Positive emotions lead to motivation, which has a strong influence on reasoning and long-term memory.

Insight 16: Front Door–Back Door

- When you write instructional objectives, make them specific, measurable, and relevant to the material being taught.
- By establishing the border of a puzzle first, you can more clearly see where the other pieces fit.

Insight 17: Peer Learning—Each One, Teach One

- If learning is driven by the inquisitive mind of a student, that learning must be met with an equally creative mind of a teacher.
- One of the best ways for students to learn a subject is to teach the content to someone.
- Each student in a group should participate equally in a group learning exercise.

- The arrangement of your classroom should allow access to every student.
- The only dumb questions are the ones that were never asked.

Insight 18: Teacher-Centered versus Student-Centered

- Students can be beautifully well-adjusted, but eventually we are all accountable for the material we have learned in order to be successful in future endeavors.

Insight 19: Use Your Teaching Energy Wisely and Stay Healthy

- It takes precious time and energy to anticipate most classroom problems. Spend your energy wisely.
- You impact students positively or negatively every single day.
- You must anticipate good days and good outcomes, rather than the opposite.
- Teacher preparation takes energy. Schedule "downtime" to recharge.
- If you're not in your classroom tomorrow, someone else will be. No teacher is indispensable.
- You are replaceable at work, but not at home.
- Doing nothing is doing something. A teacher must work at not burning the proverbial candle at both ends.
- You must show up for *you* before you can show up for others.
- Guard your energy and take care of your mind and body. You only have one of each.

Insight 20: Redirection versus Rejection

- Be careful how you speak to a student. Others are watching.
- Not all students know how to ask a question properly.

- Redirection is always a better option than rejection.

Insight 21: Develop More Than One Passion

- Stepping out of your comfort zone can improve your brain health, teaching skills, and mental health.

Insight 22: Stay Current

- As teachers, we must constantly be learning the newest methods in our craft.
- When considering an online course, study the syllabus. If it doesn't feel right, it probably isn't. Leave it alone.
- Staying current is essential, but be mindful of the added time and stress.

Insight 23: Classroom Organization and Displays

- Swap wall displays often rather than adding more to an existing display.
- You are there to teach, not preach.
- The proper arrangement of your classroom environment can be a place for optimal learning and a sanctuary of joy to practice your craft.

Insight 24: Professionalism

- Students don't want you to dress like them. They respect adults who dress like adults.
- We expect our students to be on time to class as well as with assignments. We should model this behavior.
- People are watching always. Teachers should display a high standard of conduct.

- Students expect us to act in a professional manner and are motivated by our conduct.
- Values are caught, not taught.

Insight 25: Nonverbal Cues

- The average person has over 7,000 facial expressions.
- You are the only certified teacher in the room but not the only teacher.
- Teachers have to become good actors. It is very important for a teacher to train himself to convey positive nonverbal communication.
- Nonverbal signals can help shy students communicate with the teacher.

Insight 26: Documentation

- Always document *all* interactions with parents and disciplinary events with students. A parent can argue with your memory of a child's behavior but they cannot argue with a written discipline log.

Insight 27: Parent Conferences

- Preparation prevents perspiration.
- Parents and teachers are on the same team.
- The parent has an emotional investment in their child. Keep this in mind when communicating.

Insight 28: Teacher Burnout and Rewiring Your Brain

- Find ways to express your creative skills and feel valued for the job you do and burnout may be avoided.

Insight 29: Morning Person

- When changing your sleep patterns, consistency is key.

Insight 30: Relationships with Fellow Teachers

- Teaching is a collaborative profession. Soak up all the wisdom you can from more experienced teachers.
- Toxic conversations will deplete your creative energies. Seek out positive environments and relationships.
- Be proud of your contribution to the future.

About the Author

Curt Richards is a retired public school teacher from Upstate South Carolina. He has taught various science courses for 37 years ranging from the middle school to college levels.

During his career Richards has mentored numerous teachers and practice teachers. He feels that there is no higher calling than to guide young people as well as adults through their education. In his spare time Richards enjoys studying nature, socializing with family and friends, and writing across multiple genres.

www.ingramcontent.com/pod-product-compliance
Lightning Source LLC
Chambersburg PA
CBHW030315170426
43202CB00009B/1007